Spiritual Body Building

Lessons

Kim A. Johnson

The Ministerial Association
General Conference of Seventh-day Adventists
Silver Spring, MD 20904

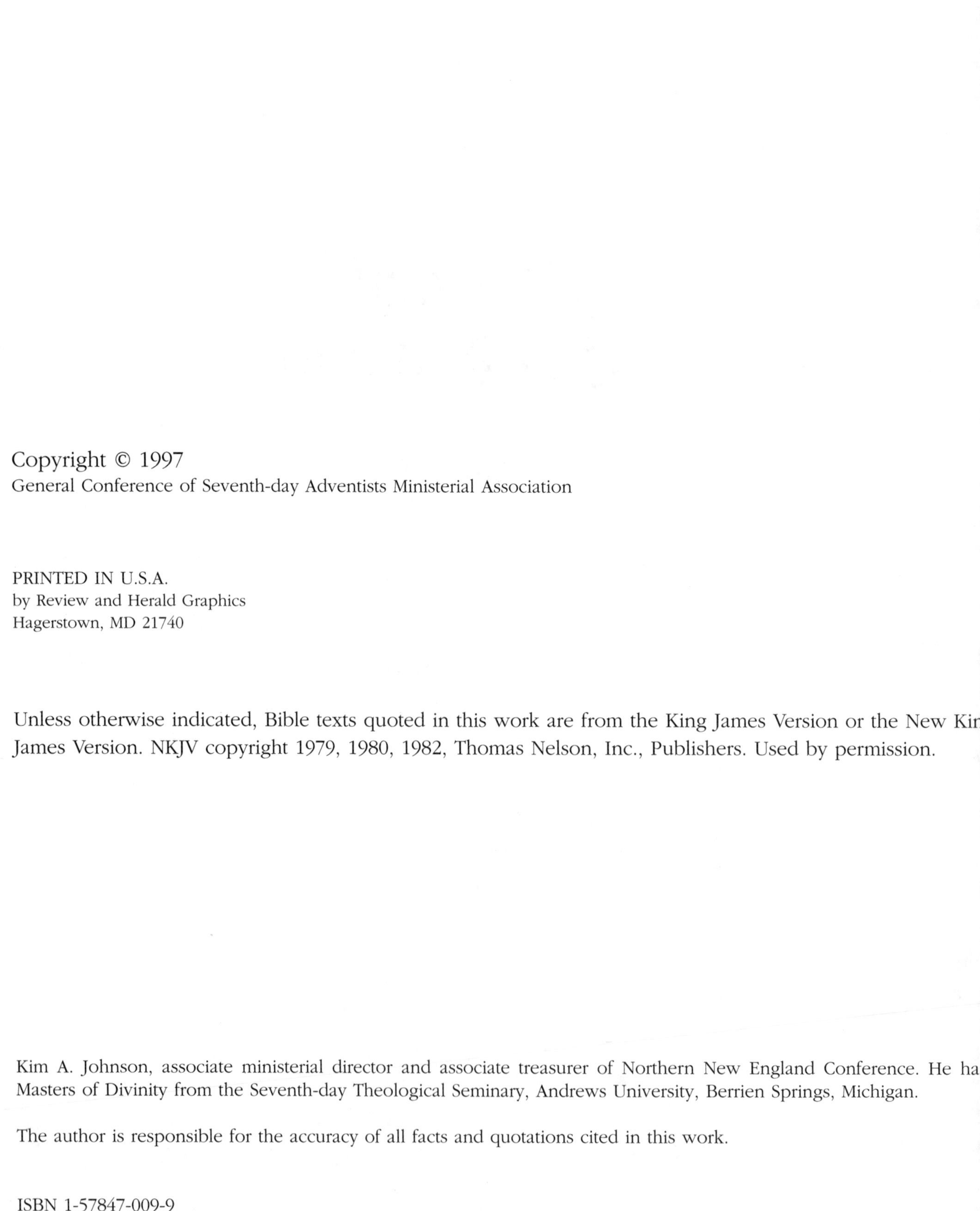

PRINTED IN U.S.A.
by Review and Herald Graphics
Hagerstown, MD 21740

Unless otherwise indicated, Bible texts quoted in this work are from the King James Version or the New Kin James Version. NKJV copyright 1979, 1980, 1982, Thomas Nelson, Inc., Publishers. Used by permission.

Kim A. Johnson, associate ministerial director and associate treasurer of Northern New England Conference. He has Masters of Divinity from the Seventh-day Theological Seminary, Andrews University, Berrien Springs, Michigan.

The author is responsible for the accuracy of all facts and quotations cited in this work.

ISBN 1-57847-009-9

Contents

Introduction

A slightly eccentric friend of mine takes great pride in never reading the instructions on how to build or fix anything. It is a carefully cultivated attitude that too often results in scrambled connections or piles of unused parts. "Doing your own thing" is no big deal when assembling a child's toy or constructing a backyard shed. It becomes a very big deal, however, when building the body of Christ. I confess to pastoring for more than a dozen years before taking the time to carefully study God's plan, His vision for how to be a church. That vision has now gripped my heart and dramatically reshaped my thinking.

I finally came to understand that we cannot be successful individual Christians until we also know how to be Christians together. A well-known author recently commented, "To be the church—our highest calling—depends on understanding the very character of the body of Christ on earth. Only then can we understand what it means to live as the people of God, serving God in today's world" (Charles Colson, *The Body*, p. 33). The Spiritual Body Building Small Group Lessons explore God's exciting vision for both you and your church. They point the way not only to greater joy in your walk with God but also to new depths of caring, fellowship, and ministry within your congregation.

Learning To Be A Group:

"A gathering of eight to twelve people does not [necessarily] constitute a group. A true group consists of a certain number of people who have committed themselves to one another and to a common goal. In essence they have agreed to struggle together . . . and care for one another." (*Growth Through Groups,* William Clemmons and Harvey Hester, p. 111)

Ice Breaker: Describe one of your best friends from your elementary school years. What did you enjoy doing together the most?

Group Activity: Remodeling a paper cup.

What is Church?

Part A

What is church? That question may seem odd. Of course we know what church is. Church is a variety of things:

- The building at 35 Main Street
- The pastor and people who meet together every Sabbath
- The worship service and Sabbath school
- All the programs we put on each year
- Church boards and elders and deacons and deaconesses

Even though such definitions sound correct, they can fall far short of capturing God's ideal. As a result of a limited understanding of what church is supposed to be, church life can become routine. Ministry can revolve around the pastor and a few overworked volunteers. More and more energy and money can be focused inward just to keep the machinery going. Members can sit in the same pews week after week and not really know the people sitting around them.

Reflection

If a group of people believe the same teachings, meet together regularly to worship and study the Bible, contribute tithes and offerings, periodically conduct various programs, and once a year elect officers, are they "church"? Why or why not?

Many churches lose their focus and clear sense of purpose. When that happens they are likely to become more of an "institution" than a biblical "church." Church as an institution can be full of activity but devoid of vitality and no longer on the cutting edge. An institution exists to perpetuate itself but is not entirely sure how or why. Has that happened to your church? Here are some questions that can help. Check yes (Y) or no (N).

1. Does most of your church budget focus on inreach (funds spent on things happening for the church

members and within the church)? ☐ Y ☐ N

2. Does most of your members' energy and ministry focus on inreach? ☐ Y ☐ N

3. Have the current ministries of your church been around for more than ten years? ☐ Y ☐ N

4. Are people chosen for church office based on their willingness to serve rather than on their spiritual gifts? ☐ Y ☐ N

5. Does most soul winning effort and visitation of members revolve around the pastor and a few members? ☐ Y ☐ N

6. Do members only infrequently bring non-Adventist visitors from your area to church? ☐ Y ☐ N

7. Is most of your church growth from transfers or the baptism of Adventist youth? ☐ Y ☐ N

8. Does change come with difficulty? ☐ Y ☐ N

9. Do almost all of your outreach efforts revolve around prepackaged programs (Breathe Free Seminars, Revelation Seminars, etc)? ☐ Y ☐ N

10. Does your church lack a clear, well-accepted sense of purpose and vision? ☐ Y ☐ N

If your answer to a majority of these questions is Yes, then your church has probably fallen into the trap of becoming institutionalized. It is now essential that you take time to discover God's plan. It is just as essential that you commit yourself to being part of that plan.

The Scriptures do not give us a specific, detailed formula for how to be church. They do, however, present us with a series of vivid mental pictures that help us form our own composite whole. Each of these pictures, or analogies, is like a piece of a puzzle. Each is essential, but incomplete. Taken together they portray the proper image. Whenever a church becomes stagnant or institutionalized, it is usually because the members have not implemented one or more of these puzzle pieces. All the pieces are exciting, and all are necessary to become "church" in the biblical sense. We will look at some of these images in this lesson and the next and leave with you the important task of discovering the rest.

1. What picture of the church does the Lord present in the following verses?

Hosea 2:19-23
2 Corinthians 11:2
Ephesians 5:25

Some people think of church as being like a club, such as the Lions or the Rotary. Club members show up at meetings, pay dues, and elect officers. Periodically the club sponsors some type of community program. But church is not a club. Neither is church a building, an institution, or a museum. The Bible pictures the church as a **bride.** It is a group of human beings intimately joined to the Bridegroom, Jesus Christ. Belonging to a church is not a matter of simply having your name on the rolls and participating in activities. Anyone who has ever been married can tell you that the marriage license is important, but it's the relationship that counts. In order for

God's people to be God's church, they need to be in relationship with Christ, the Bridegroom.

The Old Testament book Song of Solomon beautifully captures this bridal theme. In the simple yet moving account of a king who falls in love with an obscure peasant girl, we see pictured the relationship between Christ and His church. Over and over again the king's love finds expression in such phrases as,

> Behold, thou art fair my love. (4:1)
>
> Thou art beautiful, O my love. (6:4)

Here we feel the heartbeat of the Trinity. These words of affection echo the thoughts of Christ expressed in Jeremiah 31:3, "I have loved thee with an everlasting love, therefore with loving kindness I have drawn thee." And again in Ephesians 5:25, "Christ also loved the church." None of us can imagine how much Christ really cares about His church. It is beyond human comprehension. And oh, how Jesus longs to hear from His people the response of the peasant girl in the Song of Solomon, who exclaimed, "I found him whom my soul loveth!" (Song of Solomon 3:4).

Reflection

If you visited a church for several weeks, what evidence would you look for to indicate that the congregation as a whole was deeply in love with Christ? Be specific.

Jesus said some pretty remarkable things about the relationship He longs to have with each of us. In John 15:4, He gives the invitation, "Abide in Me and I in you." Then He illustrates that closeness by saying, "I am the Vine, you are the branches." We can only bud and bloom spiritually if we are connected to the Tree.

In John 17:21 Jesus offers us a mind-boggling union with the Godhead when He prays, "As thou Father art in Me and I in Thee, that they also may be one in Us." Christ is saying that the Godhead wants to be on as intimate terms with us as the members of the Godhead are with each other. Remarkable.

The Apostle Paul captures God's stirring offer of an ongoing love relationship when he counsels his readers to be "in Christ" (Romans 8:1). This is one of Paul's favorite phrases and themes, which he repeats over and over again. For Paul, being "in Christ" is similar to being "in love." It is his key to living the Christian life.

This bridal/wedding theme helps us answer the vital question, "What really is a 'successful' church in the eyes of God?" Many would define success in terms of:

- attendance on Sabbath morning
- the number of baptisms each year
- the amount of tithes and offerings
- the number of members involved in church work
- the number of community programs the church sponsors

Which, if any, of these is correct? The Apostle Paul gives us some help. When he wrote to the churches of his day he repeatedly looked for three things as sure signs of success. The Apostle defines a successful church as one that consistently manifests through its members the three qualities of faith, hope, and love (1 Corinthians

13:13; Colossians 1:4, 5; 1 Thessalonians 1:3).

It is possible for a church to be slowly dying but not realize it because the building is still there and members still attend regularly. A dying church can even look very successful as far as numbers, programs, and religious teaching are concerned. Churches can sincerely mimic God's plan. But Paul points us to the hallmarks of the real thing—the unmistakable atmosphere of Spirit-filled faith and hope, the impossible-to-counterfeit presence of a life-changing love relationship with God.

Reflection

If a group of atheists pretended to be a Christian church, with all the typical church meetings, language, prayers, and programs, how would it differ from what your church is currently doing?

---

2. **What additional picture of the church do the following verses give us?**
   2 Corinthians 6:16
   Ephesians 2:21-22
   1 Peter 2:5a

This temple is not made of brick and mortar. It is alive! It is made up of **living stones**. These stones are people whose lives are being built not by human effort or willpower, but by the Master Builder. These temple-like people have the God of love in them. They are not petty, narrow-minded, power-hungry, critical, or apathetic. They are filled with the Spirit and reveal that indwelling by being kind, patient, accepting of others, willing to serve.

Day by day God is trying to build your church into a spectacular spiritual temple far more impressive than Solomon's temple or the temple at Jerusalem. This temple is impressive because it is constructed with living stones, real people. To cooperate with God as He seeks to fit us into such a grand edifice, we need to:

- have a servant heart, willing to be placed in the building wherever He sees best
- be the kind of person others can easily get close to, as He fits the stones next to each other
- be willing and able to bear our share of the load, whether He puts us in the foundation or atop some little window
- work for the good and unity of the whole, not insisting on our own design
- remember the big picture, the larger purpose, not thinking our part is the most important

To be a spiritual temple means to abandon our independence, let down our masks, and be intimately connected with one another. Rather than being like marbles rattling around in a glass jar, we are to form close bonds of caring and involvement in other lives. We're not simply "members," but we are also friends, team members, living stones, partners in a grand and glorious enterprise.

Reflection

After the annual nominating committee report, two irate church members threaten to leave the church because they didn't get the offices they felt they deserved. Using the "living stone" principles above, how would you handle the situation? Circle as many as apply.

1. Ignore the problem.
2. Apologize for hurting their feelings.
3. Give them a Bible study on servanthood.
4. Explain the reasons to them and offer alternatives.
5. Let them have what they want in order to keep peace.
6. Refuse to give them any office because of their attitude.

Temple-like people picture church as a living organism that is growing and developing. They see church not as a place but as a process. They keep their doctrines and beliefs firm, but seek out new and better ways of doing things. They do not shun change; they embrace it. What living organism could exist without thousands of biological changes going on all the time? Change is essential for life.

A young ministerial intern in a large church finally got an opportunity to preach. At the end of his earnest sermon he felt impressed to make a rare altar call for people to accept Christ. So many people responded that he decided to forego the usual closing hymn in the interest of time. As the church members filed out, the intern was informed that the local church elders wanted to see him immediately. The young man hurried to the meeting in a side room, rejoicing in his heart that, as he supposed, the elders wanted to have a special prayer together for the new converts. When he arrived his euphoria was shattered as the head elder warned him that any more tampering with the order of service would not be tolerated.

This church had obviously drifted far from God's vision. The living stones had fossilized. They desperately needed to rediscover God's temple vision for His church.

3. What picture of the church do you find in the following verses?

John 10:27-29
Isaiah 40:11
Luke 15:3-7

Christ teaches that there is safety being within the sheepfold rather than wandering off on our own. I love Isaiah's picture of Jesus carrying us around in the security of His rugged, muscular carpenter's arms. We can depend on the wisdom and guidance of the Good Shepherd. How assuring to know that He cares so deeply for us through all the ups and downs of life.

Jesus also said, "Other sheep I have which are not of this fold: them also I must bring . . ." (John 10:16). If the church understands that it is under the leadership of the Great Shepherd, the members will be as concerned as He is about His flock, especially those who are not yet in the fold. He is desperately concerned for those other sheep. In Luke 15:3-10, Jesus talks about what He and His people will do to save those who are outside the fold: "What man . . . doth not go after that which is lost, *until he find it?"* (verse 4). God is so persistent because people are so incredibly important to Him. The word "lost" was never supposed to enter the human vocabulary. It is an awful word that fills God's heart with intense, unrelenting pain.

In his book *Good News Is For Sharing,* Leighton Ford captures a tiny bit of God's suffering:

> My little girl was lost.
>
> The certainty hit me, and I fought to keep panic away, to keep my mind clear as I reviewed the facts.

An hour and a half before, Debbie Jean had walked home from school. Thirty minutes ago, after a brief nap, she had gone out to play in the bright spring sun with her four-year-old brother, Sandy. My wife had left me with the children while she went to the store, and for some time I worked in my study upstairs. Then when I called Debbie Jean to come in, there was no answer. Sandy told me she had gone back to school. This surprised me—although Sharon School was only a few hundred yards away, across some open fields and backyards, she seldom went there to play, and never without permission.

I went to look for her in the schoolyard, but she was not there. My wife drove up as I came back home. A little uneasy, we quickly checked the five other houses on our street; she was not at any of them. A neighbor's child said he had seen her go toward school. The mute lady who lived behind us confirmed by signs that she had indeed gone through her yard. Again I walked to the school, but some children playing there had not seen her.

While my wife checked the shopping center across the street, the principal and I went through the classrooms. There was no sign of her. Now I stood on a little-used dirt road between the rear of the school and our house. I looked at the woods. It was hard to push out of my mind stories I had heard of men picking up little girls. Should we call the police? Or was there any other place she might have gone? I walked up and down the road calling "Debbie Jean," fearing the silence.

Half an hour later our little girl came walking around a corner of the school, smiling. She had gone to a candy store just beyond the school, met a friend, and gone on to her home a half mile away.

Later (when the thunder and lightning and tears were over!) I reflected on the incident. During the nearly two hours that Debbie Jean was missing, nothing else mattered. I could think of only one thing: my girl was lost. I had only one prayer, and I prayed it a thousand times, "O God, help me to find her."

But how often, I asked myself, had I felt that same terrible urgency about people in my town who were lost from God? (*Good News Is For Sharing,* Leighton Ford, p. 22-23)

Reflection

Can you identify with Leighton Ford's experience in some way through having lost someone or something precious to you? What insights can your experience provide regarding how God feels about the lost in your community?

Tell story of your lost ch.

Someone has rightly labeled God "the Hound of Heaven." He is absolutely relentless in His pursuit of the lost. When everyone else has given up the search and returned to their warm homes and busy lives, God still roams the hills, walks the back roads, and scans the horizon, calling out the names of His beloved. Even against the slimmest odds, He will die before giving up. Ask why He continues, and God would answer, "I have hope, there's still a chance."

Church is not only members talking to each other, visiting with each other, and spending their offerings on each other and their children. Church is people who share God's passion for those in their community who have never known Jesus Christ. Ministering to non-Christians is an obsession that springs from genuine, unconditional love for people. One hallmark of a truly Christian church is that it highly values and intentionally cultivates close, ongoing friendships with non-Christians and non-Adventists.

> Go to your neighbors [and associates] one by one, and come close to them till their hearts are warmed by your unselfish interest and love. (*Testimonies,* vol. 9, p. 128)

We are not all called to be evangelists or give formal Bible studies. Some ministries may be up-front and others behind the scenes. Some ministries focus on inreach and others on outreach. We dare not try to fit everyone into the same mold. We must not motivate members by guilt. Yet everyone can share a deep concern for the lost. Everyone can be part of a team that has the salvation of others as its goal. Everyone can love.

One author gives this challenging perspective:

> If you were asked what you felt was the church's number one sin or weakness, what would you say? Apathy? Too much secularism? Too much social gospel? Too worldly? Too liberal? Too conservative? If I were asked this question, I would say that I feel our major weakness is that we have become too program centered rather than people centered. Jesus loved people and used programs. He always discerned what the individual's need was first and adjusted His program or ministry to meet that person's need—never the other way around. Unless we make a conscious effort to put people first, we may unwittingly love our programs our doctrine, our beliefs, and even our Bible more than we love people. (*I Hate Witnessing,* p. 105)

Reflection

What do you think the author is getting at when he warns that we can love our doctrine and our Bible more than we love people? That we should be filled with the spirit.

If we love programs more than people, we can become like the hospital that gives everyone the same treatment no matter what the ailment. It is too easy to plan our outreach solely based on a limited list of prepackaged programs, rather than listening to the true needs of the community. Too often I have sat on personal ministries committees where the conversation went something like this: "We haven't done any outreach at all for so long. Don't you think we ought to do something? Hey, why don't we try one of those programs that Fred did two years ago; he's so good at it. Only church members turned out, but it did us all good."

Success is defined as simply conducting the program, whether or not it actually scratches where non-Adventists itch. Relatively speaking, few sheep will be rescued by such a rigid, one-size-fits-all approach. Sheep are still found mostly one by one among the rocks, hills, and valleys.

We often overlook another aspect of shepherding. It doesn't do much good for the church to find a lost sheep and then let it get lost all over again. We can seem far more concerned about people *before* they are baptized than *afterward*. Perhaps we feel that once we have "made the sale" we can move on to the next customer. I remember one longtime church member commenting, "Hey, nobody coddled me after I joined this church twenty-five years ago. Nobody baby-sat me, and I made it. Why can't they? I'm here at church every Sabbath. Never miss. They just don't make church members like they used to!" As a result of such callous thinking, many lost people join the church only to wander off again a few years later.

> Picture a twenty-four-year-old mother, Diane, who has just given birth to her first child, baby Jessica. After about an hour, Jessie is brought into Mom's hospital room for feeding. The nurse lays the precious little bundle on the clean pink sheets next to mommy. Diane glances down at the baby and then back at the nurse with a look of bewilderment. The nurse asks politely, "Is there something I can help you with?" Diane replies, "There sure is! What's this kid doing in here?" The nurse offers kindly, "Well, it's time for Jessie to get some num nums." Diane shoots back, "Num nums? I did my part by giving birth. Now all I want to do is rest up a little and head home—alone. I've got a lot of stuff to catch up on. This pregnancy has been very time-consuming. You probably think pregnancy is a piece of cake, don't you? Believe me, it's not. If Jessica needs milk or a diaper change, that's your problem. My part's done."

Crazy, of course. Any good parent knows that 98 percent of the hard work happens after birth, especially from ages 13-16! Simply defining success by how many baptisms a church has is like defining successful parenting by how many babies a couple produces. At baptism, the church's work has only begun.

Reflection

Someone defined his own church as "a place where we all come to be lonely together." A member of another congregation commented, "In a church where everyone appears strong, no one grows." Which of these two statements do you feel best captures the reason so many people leave the Seventh-day Adventist church? Explain.

The Trinity wants to team up with us to make it simple to be saved tough as nails to be lost. God embraces sinners quickly and lets go with infinite reluctance. God designs that before anyone leaves His fold, they must first crash through several huge barriers: the Spirit, the cross, the Gospel, conscience, truth—and us.

Review Questions

1. If Christ were to write a love letter to your church, His bride, what would it say?

2. Your non-Christian neighbors invite you to their home, for the first time, to attend the husband's birthday party. There will be drinking and dancing. What will you do and why?

3. How many people in your church would you really feel comfortable confiding in if you happened to be going through serious personal difficulty? What was the basis for your selection?

Love in Action

My Choice:

Sit by some lonely person in church this week and help him or her feel like an important part of God's flock.

Your Choice:

Learning to be a Group: "Active listening" means giving people your full attention while they are talking and making an effort to listen for the meaning and feeling *behind* their words. Concentrate on what *they* are saying rather than simply waiting for a chance to share your own thoughts.

Love in Action Feedback: Did you find a lonely person in church last Sabbath to encourage?

Ice Breaker: In what direction of the compass—north, south, east, or west—have you traveled the farthest? What experience was the most enjoyable and/or most memorable?

Group Activity: (Write group members' answers on large paper with felt marker.)

- What does your local church currently do "very well"?
- Where could your church improve the most?

(Save the large paper and review it again after studying all the lessons in this series.)

What is Church?

Part B

In our previous lesson we dealt with the biblical pictures of the church as the bride, living stones, and flock. In this lesson we will continue to explore what the Bible has to say about church.

> Suppose you have been envisioning your dream house. For years you've made plans in your mind and on paper. The design incorporates your thoughtful attention to every detail, makes incredibly efficient use of space, and takes advantage of the latest advances in construction. An architect carefully draws up blueprints. Now it's time to hire a builder. You eventually give him the blueprints, drawing his attention to several critical areas. Because you have to be away on a business trip for a while, you tell him to please give you a call if there are any questions. After returning a month later you anxiously drive out to the building site. The foundation is in and the home is fully framed in. To your astonishment the house looks very different from the one you envisioned. Immediately you phone the contractor and ask, "What happened? That house is nothing like what I had in mind. The blueprints spelled it all out!" He replies casually, "Hey, blueprints really slow me down. I just rely on what I think is best. I kinda like the way it came out myself."

How would you react? You'd fire the guy. And yet, how often we are much like that builder. We organize a church (I'm not talking about the building here) and get a busy round of programs going, yet rarely consult God's blueprint for what church should be. God's plan may not be as detailed as a blueprint, but He's given plenty of instruction.

Are you sure the way you conduct church, the way you are church, conforms to the biblical plan? Your answer is critical in determining whether or not your church will accomplish God's glorious purpose.

1. **What is the next picture that the Scriptures present of the church?**

   Romans 12:4-5
   Ephesians 4:11-12, 15-16
   1 Corinthians 12:4-27

   Picture of the body parts.
   Different ministries in the church -

In these verses the Apostle Paul compares the church members and their spiritual gifts to the parts of a **body**. Some members are fingernails, others are ears. Some are feet, others eyes. Can you imagine a body that has only two or three parts that are fully developed? Big arms and shriveled legs. Huge ears and puny hands. An enormous mouth and tiny heart. What a bizarre individual. But that's exactly how churches look when they do not develop all the talents and abilities of members. That's how churches look when they focus on one or two aspects of ministry, such as reaping, to the exclusion of the great variety of ministries available.

Just as human bodies cannot function well without cooperation and unity of purpose, neither can a church.

> Suppose that a lazy, out-of-shape guy thinks about getting some much-needed exercise. As the message to exercise travels from his brain throughout his system, 90 percent of his body votes to take a brisk nature walk south, but the other 10 percent of his body votes to go north. And suppose the 10 percent minority raises a real stink about the vote—how unfair it was and how manipulative the other body parts were. Soon the 10 percent begins to lobby other body parts in an attempt to win them over—"Hey, liver, you know the pancreas is out to lunch on this thing!" The minority becomes more critical and more adamant until the body is torn with strife. Some body parts threaten to leave if they don't get their way. Eventually there is so much confusion that the person winds up lying down on the couch, munching potato chips, and watching soaps and re-runs on TV.

This scenario is not much different from what happens in too many churches. If the church is to function like a healthy body, individuals must surrender their pet peeves, hobby horses, personal agendas, and stubborn independence for the good of the whole.

When a church loses sight of God's vision for an integrated body, that church can become like the board that voted to buy a new church broom—and then wrangled for three hours trying to decide where to keep it.

Paul emphasizes that members should work hard at creating unity within Christ's body. Note his important counsel:

> Make every effort to keep the unity of the Spirit through the bond of peace. (Ephesians 4:3)

> I appeal to you, brothers, in the name of our Lord Jesus Christ, that all of you agree with one another so that there may be no divisions among you and that you may be perfectly united in mind and thought. (1 Corinthians 1:10)

Paul is simply expanding on Jesus' deepest heart longing for His church, "That they may be one, even as We are one" (John 17:22). God's grand design is that His church reflect the love and unity that exists within the Godhead. Can you imagine God the Father fighting with Christ? Can you picture the Holy Spirit gossiping about Jesus? Impossible.

Ray C. Stedman underscores this vital point when he writes,

> It is extremely important that Christians stop quarreling, bickering [and] struggling against one another. . . . A church where these attitudes exist is a totally ineffective body in its community. Such a church can say nothing to which the world will pay any attention. (*Body Life,* p. 34)

Reflection

Does any church member have the right to push a personal agenda to the point that other members begin to take sides? What if that person says they have biblical "proof"? (see 1 Corinthians 12:25) X Discuss.

The New Testament gives us wonderful insights into how the body of Christ should function by using a certain phrase over and over—"one another." The Bible writers use the phrase "one another" to point out specific activities that will enable the church to be a true body. This phrase occurs 58 times in the New Testament (*Building Up One Another*, Gene Getz). The Scriptures tell us to:

- *Be devoted* to one another (Romans 12:10)
- *Honor* one another (Romans 12:10)
- Be of the *same mind* with one another (Romans 15:5)
- *Accept* one another (Romans 15:7)
- *Greet* one another (Romans 16:3-6, 16)
- *Serve* one another (Galatians 5:13)
- *Bear* one another's burdens (Galatians 6:2)
- *Submit* to one another (Ephesians 5:21)
- *Encourage* one another (1 Thessalonians 5:11)

Can you imagine how wonderful it would be if a church committed itself to live by these principles? Obviously such a church would put people first. As one writer has indicated, we are not in the church growth business, we are in the people growth business.

The Apostle Paul uses this same phrase again in Romans 12:5 (NASB), where he shares a very important truth: "So we who are many, are one body in Christ, and individually members one of another."

Paul's point is that the members of the body of Christ should be as interdependent as are the different parts of the human body. Individual church members cannot function effectively by themselves. The Bible cannot conceive of someone having an effective relationship with Christ the Head without also having an effective relationship with His body, the church.

Reflection

Can you recall when you personally experienced, through someone else, any of the "one another" texts listed above? (For example, "accept one another" or "encourage one another.") Why was that important to you at that time? At Ole-Bola in Nigeria.

---

2. What picture of the church do you find in the following text:

Matthew 5:13 Salt

The Old Testament Israelites often distorted God's plan terribly and chose to isolate themselves from the world.

For many years they put up high ethnic walls and concentrated almost exclusively on avoiding contamination from nonbelievers. In the New Testament Jesus tries to correct that imbalance and compares the church to **salt**.

It is vital that Christians come apart with fellow believers to recharge their spiritual batteries. But that should never become an end in itself. God has chosen us for service. God commissions His followers to get out of the saltshaker and mingle, like salt, with the world.

> The church, like the circulation of the blood in the human body, is constantly on the move. It gathers for inspiration and instruction as the blood gathers in the heart and lungs for oxygenation and cleansing. It is then pumped out into the world just as the blood carries nutrients, hormones, and enzymes to the most distant parts of the body. You cannot go to church; you are the church wherever you go. (*The Equipping Pastor,* R. Paul Stevens, p. 126-7)

How would you feel about an ambulance crew who never left the station for fear of being contaminated by someone's illness? Suppose their only response to emergency phone calls was to invite sick people to attend first aid classes at the station every Tuesday evening. Isn't it just as inappropriate for us to repeatedly ask people to come to us and our programs rather than going to them and trying to understand their needs?

> We are not to wait for souls to come to us; we must seek them out where they are. *(Christ's Object Lessons,* p. 229)

Reflection

If your local church ceased to exist tomorrow, what would the non-Adventists in your community miss the most?

A noted Adventist teacher and author commented,

> God's mission is always accomplished through incarnation. No program, institution, or communications satellite will do much good unless the world sees the gospel of Christ exemplified through His own people in their daily lives—in the way they have solved the daily problems of self and society, in their service to their fellowmen, and in the genuine Christian fellowship of the community of faith. (*Mission Possible,* Gottfried Oosterwal, Southern Publishing Association, 1972, p. 73)

Years ago, at the height of racial tension in the South, a young white preacher decided to take Jesus' salt and incarnation strategy seriously. He became an unofficial chaplain to the local chapter of the Ku Klux Klan. Though he detested all the Klan stood for, the preacher visited the Klan members regularly, ate at their tables, tended to their sick, emptied their bed pans, attended their parties, and buried their dead. The young man's own church members were appalled by their pastor's efforts. He explained that Klan members would turn a deaf ear to traditional evangelistic methods and that only Christlike love could break through their towering wall of hate. Over the next few months, he himself became the object of stinging gossip from church people. Christian friends abandoned him.

If salt is to permeate society it must mingle with it, be incarnated as part of it, without being overcome.

The story is told of a little town in France whose only major industry was a perfume factory that employed people from all over the countryside. At five o'clock, when the whistle blew for quitting time, the workers filtered back to their own villages and homes. Tourists often commented how the presence of these factory workers made the whole area smell so beautiful. So often we try to avoid being "soiled" by the world, forgetting that we have a mission. How can we "perfume" society if we run from it?

3. What is another important picture of the church?
Ephesians 6:10-20

While writing the book of Ephesians, Paul is under house arrest. In daily contact with Roman soldiers, the apostle pictures in his mind's eye a spiritual **army**, the church of God. Their battle is not primarily with human beings, but with the devil and his forces of spiritual darkness.

> The apostle [pictures] vast armies of evil gathered together to overwhelm the church. The contest is desperately uneven, with all the advantages on the side of the enemy, except as the church makes an alliance, through faith, with the resources of Omnipotence. (*Seventh-day Adventist Bible Commentary,* vol. 6, p. 1043)

We have David and Goliath all over again. Few churches realize they are under very real spiritual attack. Evil angels meet regularly to plot and plan how to bring ruin. The devil's most effective weapon is not usually persecution. Instead, infighting, busyness, apathy, or lack of vision will do just fine.

Reflection

Evil angels are plotting how to weaken your church spiritually. What strategy would be most effective for them to employ? Choose one.

1. Start a fight between two key church families.
2. Let the church be run by a few dictatorial people.
3. Keep the leaders "majoring in minors."
4. Make everyone comfortable with the status quo.
5. Have a bunch of drug addicts from the streets start attending church.

Paul's counsel to God's army, the church, is filled with encouragement. In Ephesians 6:10 he says, "Be strong in the Lord." A better translation is, "Be made powerful in the Lord." God quite literally wants to pour His power into the church, if it is willing to receive. The Apostle concludes verse 10 by describing this power as "the power of *His* might." God is the source. The Greek word here for power is "dunamis," from which we get our word "dynamite." That is the same word Paul used back in Ephesians 1:19, where he wrote about, "the exceeding greatness of His power to usward." God doesn't just have power; it is exceeding power. God has made every provision for His army on earth to triumph gloriously.

One of my favorite verses regarding God's power is in Matthew 28. Christ is in the tomb and a huge, sealed stone lies across the entrance. Roman soldiers stand guard. Evil angels blanket the entire area. Then Matthew tells us,

> And there was a great earthquake, for the angel of the Lord descended from heaven, and came and rolled back the stone from the door, and sat upon it. (Matthew 28:3)

Just one angel scatters all the opposition! And then, after removing the stone, "he sat upon it"? The angel turned a major obstacle into a comfortable resting place. That's power.

As part of his house arrest, Paul is handcuffed to a Roman soldier. Day after day the two are chained at the wrist. Suppose the soldier smelled bad, talked incessantly, or slept all the time and snored? What a pain that would have been for the Apostle. In such a circumstance, Paul became very familiar with Roman battle dress. He mentions the soldier's various articles of clothing, in the order in which they would be put on, and gives them each a spiritual meaning. Twice he urges us to put on the "whole armor" of God, not to pick and choose what we think we need (Ephesians 6:11, 13). He then talks about the armor, piece by piece:

- having your loins girt about with [the belt of] truth
- having on the breastplate of righteousness
- your feet shod with the preparation of the gospel of peace
- taking the shield of faith
- take the helmet of salvation
- and take the sword of the Spirit

Truth, righteousness, the gospel of peace, faith, salvation, and the Spirit—powerful outfit! Every provision has been made for His church, and you, to conquer.

In Romans 1:16 Paul talks about another aspect of God's power that is vital for the church. He writes, "For I am not ashamed of the gospel of Christ, for it is the power of God unto salvation." The gospel is the good news about a God who sacrifices Himself. The gospel defines true power as the spirit of self-sacrifice and servanthood. Paul elaborates on this theme in Philippians 2:9, where he tells us that because Jesus gave Himself so fully, "God has exalted [Him] to the highest rank and power" (*Seventh-day Adventist Bible Commentary*, vol. 7, p. 156). Christ's great power came as a result of great humiliation.

Jesus spanned the greatest distance in the universe, from the throne to the cross. According to Paul, that incredible journey had seven crucial downward steps:

though He was in the form of God
did not count equality with God a thing to be grasped
but emptied Himself
taking the form of a servant
being born in the likeness of men
he became obedient unto death
even the death on a cross. (Philippians 2:6-8)

He then concludes, "Let this mind be in you which was also in Christ Jesus" (Philippians 2:5). The soldiers in God's army are mighty precisely because they are willing to put others first. They don't covet power or demand it; they are given power because they serve.

Reflection

Which of the following abuses of power and influence by local church leaders can be the most harmful to a congregation? Choose two and explain.

a. Spreading false rumors about members with whom they don't agree.
b. Letting people know they would get very upset if not put back in office.

c. Dominating discussions and deliberations in order to get their way.
d. Manipulating others through guilt or intimidation.
e. "Doing their own thing" and refusing to take advice.

---

4. What is our final Scriptural picture of the church?
Ephesians 3:14-15

What a rich picture of the church—a **family.** The word "family" brings to mind such wonderful images and welcome feelings. Of all the ways the Scriptures portray the church, this is perhaps the warmest and most intimate.

First of all, family is designed by God to be a **safe** haven. No matter how awful your day has been, the family will be glad you're home. You can be yourself. No masks, no pretensions, free from harshness, put-downs, and gossip.

Family is also a source of fierce **loyalty**. Let an outsider criticize a family member and the others will pounce on him. They will defend and support each other to the death, literally.

Family also provides **acceptance**. You belong. You are loved no matter what. You fit in.

Reflection

In what ways is it possible for a barroom to be more like God's plan for church than church is?

In these first two lessons we have briefly examined several biblical pictures of church:

- Bride
- Living Stones
- Flock
- Body
- Salt
- Army
- Family

All these puzzle pieces begin to form a picture that is, in a sense, larger than the sum of its many parts. These pieces also help us understand the most important biblical concept of church—**the glory of God**. Like spokes in a wheel, each of the biblical images of church points toward the hub, God's glory, which is His character of love.

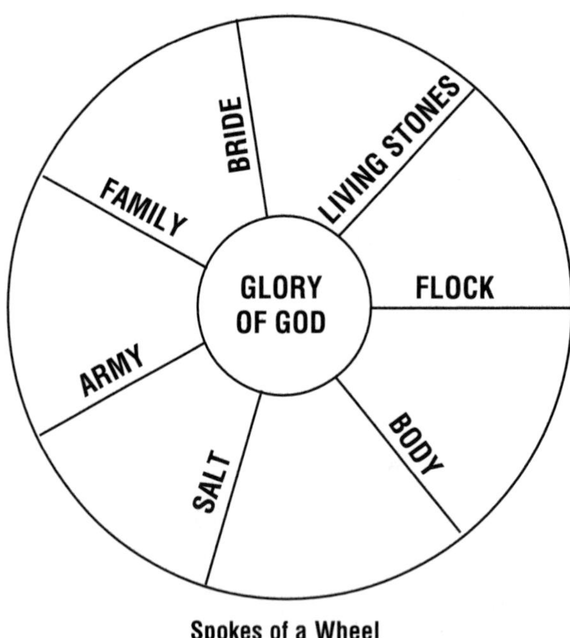

Spokes of a Wheel

Of all the New Testament writers, Paul expounds the theme of God's glory best, especially in Ephesians. In Ephesians 3:14-21, Paul expresses his deepest desire for the church at Ephesus—that they reveal God's love. (Since this letter was most likely a general epistle, the Apostle's heart longing really takes in all the Christians in Asia Minor.) He realizes how profoundly God's glory could be seen in these church members if they would:

- be strengthened with might by the Spirit in the inner man (verse 16)
- [let] Christ dwell in [their] hearts by faith (verse 17)
- be rooted and grounded in love (verse 18)
- comprehend . . . the breadth and length and depth and height [of the] love of Christ which passes knowledge (verses 18, 19)
- be filled with all the fulness of God (verse 19)

What a list. And what a vision for the church. Paul then talks about the source of all these wonderful things: "Now unto Him that is able to do exceeding abundantly above all that we ask or think, according to the power that worketh in us . . ." (Ephesians 3:20).

> Suppose you are sitting in a huge jet plane and the stewardess comes over and asks, "How high would you like to fly today?" You reply nervously, "I'm not sure how powerful this jet really is or how much I can trust the pilot. Let's just taxi around the runway." So the engines are revved up and the plane is skillfully motored all around the airport. The stewardess stops by once again to see how you are doing, and you exclaim, "Great flight, huh!" She looks a little puzzled and replies, "Well, we never really left the ground at all. Why don't you let us take you a little higher this time?" Your confidence is up a little, so you agree reluctantly. This time the plane slowly circles over the airport and lands easily. Apart from the four times you ran up and down the aisle yelling, "We're all going to die!" the flight went well. Finally after several flights, you have enough confidence to say, "Hey, I trust you guys. Take me up as high as you want."

In Ephesians, Paul is describing a spiritual flight higher than human thought can reach. God can get us there if we choose to trust. He is *more* than able.

Review Questions

1. The church is pictured in Scripture as a bride, living stones, flock, body, salt, army, and family. Which picture stood out most in your mind? Why?

2. Five years from now the local newspaper will have a front-page article about your church. What is in the photo? What do you want the article to emphasize?

3. List three specific things your church might do to strengthen the sense of community and oneness among the members.

4. Do you see any difference in importance between the biblical doctrine of the Sabbath and the doctrine of what "church" is supposed to be? Why is one emphasized so much more than the other?

Love in Action

My Choice:

Think of three people outside your group to whom you'd like to send an Encouragement/Appreciation Card. Each card would contain words of support and/or an expression of thankfulness for something they have done.

Your Choice:

Learning to be a Group: Participate, don't dominate. It is helpful not to talk too much or too little. Monitor yourself. Help people who are more shy and reserved to feel comfortable sharing. Strive for equality of input. Also, take time to read the lesson carefully ahead of time rather than cramming at the last minute. You will get out of the group what you put in.

Love in Action Feedback: Share something about your Encouragement/Appreciation Cards.

Ice Breaker: Please read this before the upcoming meeting! We're going to do Show & Tell. Bring something this week from your home to show the group (other than a photo). Choose something that has special meaning for you.

You are a Minister!

Would you hire a "layman" to take out your appendix? Would you hire a "layman" to build your dream house? Probably not, because we want such important things done by a *professional.* The dictionary defines a *layman* as someone "who is not an expert." In other words, an amateur. No one wants an amateur doing surgery or building houses because they might make a mess of things.

Interestingly, that is just the way the church of the Middle Ages defined regular church members. They called them "laymen," amateurs at church work. Church members were thought of as being amateurs at spirituality, amateurs at praying and Bible study. Not very adept. The laymen were people who lived and worked "in the world" and were therefore not very holy. Back in those days, the laymen were contrasted with the clergy, who were experts in spiritual things. The clergy were the experts at praying, teaching the Word, and the work of the church in general. Thus there developed two distinct classes in the church of the Middle Ages—the inferior, amateurish "laymen" and the holy, spiritually superior "clergy." This dichotomy between clergy and laymen was, unfortunately, totally unscriptural.

It was Martin Luther who finally reacted forcefully against this false teaching. He wrote, "Christ does not have two bodies or two different kinds of body, one temporal and one spiritual. . . . Whoever has undergone baptism may boast that he is already a priest" (*Mission Possible*, Gottfried Oosterwal, p. 105). Did you notice how Luther referred to laypeople? He had the audacity to call them priests. That took tremendous courage at a time when priests were all-powerful and saw any erosion of their power as heresy. This concept of ordinary church members actually being priests in the eyes of God was a root cause of the Protestant Reformation. This powerful truth freed people to believe they could study the Bible on their own and be saved by praying directly to God in faith. This doctrine of the priesthood of all believers swept through Europe in the 1500s and 1600s, changing the lives of thousands of people. It liberated them spiritually, just as if they had been released from a dark and dreary dungeon.

Luther did not dream this doctrine up. He found it in 1 Peter 2:9, where we read, "You are a chosen generation, a royal priesthood, a holy nation, a peculiar people; that you should show forth the praises of him who has called you out of darkness into His marvelous light."

When Peter penned these words two thousand years ago, he was sharing one of the most revolutionary truths imaginable. To put Peter's revolution in perspective, we need to go back and visit the Israel of his day. In Peter's time there were probably about 7,500 Jewish priests living in and around Palestine. The priests were considered a class all by themselves. They were held in high esteem by the rest of Judaism and looked upon as special. We can hardly imagine today the great spiritual gap the average Israelite felt between himself and the priests.

The priests were so anxious to make sure common Israelites didn't interfere that some of the Levites were designated as temple police to keep ordinary people outside the priestly temple court. The only things the common people were expected to do were (1) show up at major religious functions and (2) bring the correct offerings. Sound familiar?

Now if the priest was miles above the average Israelite, he was infinitely above the Gentiles. For a priest to even touch a Gentile made him unclean.

> The story is told in Jewish writings of a certain high priest who planned to officiate on the Day of Atonement. He was particularly careful the seven days before the great event to avoid becoming ritually unclean. This was the high point of his year and the high point of Israel's year as well. Under special guard he was meticulous in his preparation and watchfulness. But with just twelve hours to go before the big day, the high priest had to be disqualified because on an evening walk he accidentally stepped on some Gentile spit.

As far as the priests were concerned, Gentiles were crude beings, almost animals, spiritual fools, far more sinful than the worst Israelite and good for nothing but fuel for the fires of hell.

It was against this background that the Apostle Peter dared to write 1 Peter 2:9. The book of 1 Peter was written to be circulated among Jewish converts to be sure, but its primary target audience was Christian Gentiles. Gentiles, mind you! As his stylus moved across the parchment, Peter overthrew 1,400 years of sacred teaching. In a few strokes of the pen, he completely overturned the Jewish system, pointed a finger at his stunned Gentile readers, and called them priests. "You are now a royal priesthood. . . ." The most unsophisticated, simpleminded Gentile Christian is now equal in spiritual standing with the great rabbis of Israel.

Reflection

After studying Scripture, a Gentile Christian in the days of Peter still cannot accept the fact that he is now a full-fledged priest before God. What can be done to help him? Choose one.

1. Elect him to the church board.
2. Give him more personal Bible study.
3. Bring him into your own circle of friends.
4. Ask him where he would like to serve in the church.
5. Give him some audio tapes on the topic by a powerful preacher.
6. Put him in a small group with some church members who are former Pharisees.

The New Testament Christians embraced Peter's vision of church. As a result, the Gospel spread through the civilized world like wildfire. Notice how this phenomenal growth was accomplished:

> The Christianity that conquered the Roman empire was not an affair of brilliant preachers addressing packed congregations. . . . When we try to picture how it was done, we see domestic servants teaching Christ in and through their domestic service, workers doing it through their work, small shopkeepers through their trade, and so on, rather than eloquent propagandists swaying mass meetings of interested inquirers. It was a lay movement . . . . There were different ministries according to the gifts bestowed upon them. (*Mission Possible,* Gottfried Oosterwal, p. 107)

Peter would eventually be murdered, nailed to a tree, partly because he taught this radically new vision of "church." Unfortunately, as far as too many modern church members are concerned, Peter died for nothing. Many churches today fail to follow Peter and Luther's lead. Clergy are still seen as being somehow more spiritual than the average member.

"Why, we'd never do that," you say. "We'd never think like those people back in the Middle Ages." Don't be too sure. Do any of the following examples have a familiar ring?

> Example 1: A pastor returned home after being away for three days. He learned that an elderly church member was in the hospital having some elective surgery. He called the head elder to get the particulars first and then that afternoon stopped by the hospital for a visit. No sooner had he entered the church member's room than she began to complain that no minister had come to see her yet. After letting her run out of steam, the pastor leaned over her bed and commented, "Well, I was told by the head elder that you have been visited by no less than ten ministers in the last two days." "That's ridiculous," she countered, "I'd recognize a minister if I saw one!" Then the pastor began to list the names. "Well, Fred and his wife stopped by. And there's Jane, Bob, Peter, Susan. . . ." "No, no," the lady protested, "they're just laymen!"

Just laymen. Sadly, this statement reflects the thinking of many church members today—"Unless the pastor visits me, I didn't really get a spiritual visit, at least not a professional one." Where did such thinking come from? Certainly not the Scriptures. We are not all pastors, but every Christian is a minister.

> Example 2: A church member who was concerned about an ailing loved one asked her pastor, "Would you please pray for Mary? I know your prayers really work." Somehow she thought that his prayers were more effective than those of an ordinary church member. He supposedly had an inside track.

> Example 3: Many churches will not begin the Sabbath potluck dinner until the pastor has said grace. One church actually let the food get cold while the deacons chased around the church looking for the pastor who was counseling someone in a side room.

> Example 4: Too many church members expect the pastor to attend every committee meeting held in the church, or at least most of them. If the pastor is not present, they accuse him of not being interested or say the meeting was not "official."

In many churches, tragically, the pastor has become the primary shepherd, soul winner, fund raiser, organizer, administrator, and errand boy. According to the New Testament, however, it is actually the members in the pews who are to be the primary shepherds of the flock and the primary soul winners. Notice how seriously the Spirit of Prophecy treats this topic:

> It is a fatal mistake to suppose that the work of saving souls depends alone on the ordained minister. . . . All who receive the life of Christ are ordained to work for the salvation of their fellowmen. (*The Desire of Ages,* p. 822)

The term "laymen" comes from the Greek word "laos." The scriptural meaning of laos is "a special people." It refers to *all* Christians, including the pastor. So, biblically, the pastor is a layman. People and pastor together make up the laity. In Scripture, to be called a member of the laity is a wonderful compliment. In the eyes of God you are very special.

Many centuries of wrong thinking have made the non-pastoral members of the laity feel as though their ministry is less significant than that of pastors. Not so. The scholar/pastor John R. W. Stott offers this perspective:

> There must be many of us in the Church . . . who need to perform a complete mental somersault. It is not the clergyman who is the really important person and the other layman a rather inferior brand of churchman, but the other way round. It is the [non-pastors] who are important, the whole Church serving both God and man, the vanguard of Christ's army as it advances to the conquest of the world. . . ." (*One People,* J. R. W. Stott, p. 48)

The rest of the laity are not mandated to simply do what the pastor doesn't feel like doing; rather, they have vital ministries in their own right. R. Paul Stevens points the way for the whole laity to discover their special places in God's kingdom:

> Perhaps a nonclergy layperson reading this might think, "I'm really quite happy to come to church and to be fed by my pastor. I appreciate his ministry, and I'm glad to assist him in any way I can." But, Mr., Ms. or Mrs. Layperson, I ask on the authority of the New Testament, "Have you forgotten who you are? You are a minister of Jesus Christ, a holy priest, an ambassador for Christ, an agent of reconciliation in the world, salt and light and yeast." (*Equipper's Guide to Every-Member Ministry,* p. 10)

Every follower of Christ is a full-time minister. As a "layman," you are a priest to your world—whether it be in the home, job, society, supermarket, auto repair shop, or neighbor's house. You are *called.* You are a key part of God's plan. No more carving life into sacred or secular. Everything you do is now part of your sacred ministry for God.

Reflection

Is it more sacred for a pastor to preach a sermon or for a Christian plumber to fix a leaky pipe? Which work is more "priestly"?

A church in Connecticut decided to take seriously the biblical concept that every Christian is a priest to his or her world. In harmony with this emphasis, during certain church services they set workers apart for their calling. For instance, the electricians in the congregation were invited to be present for a special dedication ceremony. On the communion table they placed a unique visual reminder of their profession made of coils of wire and several tools. They were asked to come down front for the following commissioning prayer:

> Creator God, You are the source of all Energy and Power. We bring before You this day those who work with the power of electricity, who seek to channel, transform, and convert a dangerous energy into power for good. Guard them and keep them safe. Give them patience with tracking problems to their source, and caution in their work. And grant them a sense of ministry in their making our lives safe, in their striving for excellence, in their dealings with people. In the name of Jesus. Amen. (*The Empowering Church,* Davida Foy Crabtree, p. 6)

Another church service focused on the hairdressers in the congregation. Their visual reminder on the communion table included hair dryers, brushes, and wigs. They were dedicated to their priestly calling with this prayer:

> Creator and creating God, we raise before You in prayer all who work as hairdressers, barbers, and beauticians, who by their creativity and skill seek to help people feel good about themselves. Be present to them and grant them patience in their many interactions with the public and co-workers. Grant them a sense of ministry in their listening to the lonely and hurting, in their ability to transform mundane interactions into meaningful relationships, in their ability to give joy and feelings of self-worth simply by their work. In the name of Jesus. Amen. (*The Empowering Church*, Davida Foy Crabtree, p. 6-7)

We desperately need a "theology of work" in order for our church members to have confidence that the labor they expend from Sunday through Friday, in the home or community, is truly a ministry for God. They are working for God just as surely as the pastor is. We often limit being "witnesses at work" to sharing a Bible text. But it is much more than that. We can be powerful witnesses for Christ through our excellence, attitude, fairness, dedication, innovation, helpfulness, and team spirit. We can infect our workplace with the principles of the God's kingdom.

Sabbath morning teaching and preaching needs to be geared more directly to helping these marketplace priests be effective in their calling. Sabbath morning should be linked clearly to Monday morning by providing practical Scriptural answers to these questions: "How can a Christian deal effectively with an unreasonable boss?" "How do you handle boredom?" "What do you do when you feel you've been unfairly passed over for a promotion?" "How can you tell if a fellow worker is open to the Spirit?"

Things have become so twisted over the centuries that even our use of the word "clergy" is a misnomer. In Scripture, the Greek "kleros" are all of God's people. *You* are a member of the clergy. Isn't it amazing how mixed up things have become? Biblically, you can say that the clergy are laymen and laymen are clergy.

The picture is further muddied by the fact that in Scripture there is a spiritual gift, or ability, called "Pastor." This means that some people in the pews may have the gift of pastoring. The paid pastor may not be the only pastor in the congregation. In that case we would have the head pastor and what some call lay pastors.

In summary then,

- every Christian is a **minister**, and
- everyone is a member of the **laity**, and
- everyone is a member of the **clergy**, and
- everyone actually does ministry **full time**.

In its early history the Adventist Church clearly understood Peter's dramatic teaching on the priesthood of all believers. As a result, from 1870 to 1900 the Seventh-day Adventist membership increased a phenomenal 432 percent. After 1901, when the biblical concept of the priesthood of all believers became blurred, a sharp drop occurred—from 1900 to 1930 the church grew by only 184 percent. From 1930 to 1960 it again dropped to 167 percent (*Mission Possible*, Gottfried Oosterwal, p. 107). The key to rekindling the tremendous growth of the early years is to discover again the wonderful truth that you are a priest.

Kent Hunter provides this hopeful insight:

> One of the greatest teachings that came out of the Reformation was a re-emphasis of the New Testament principle of the royal priesthood of all believers. Whenever the Christian movement has taken on vitality, it has re-captured

this important grass roots notion. (*Moving the Church Into Action,* Kent Hunter, p. 46)

Reflection

From what you've learned so far, how do you react to the concept that you are a minister and priest? Choose one answer and tell why.

a. I'm paid to do my job, and we pay the pastor to do his. Frankly, I still think the pastor should be the primary shepherd and soul winner.
b. This is all very new to me, and I feel a little confused.
c. I'm sick of being a second class church member! I'm excited to know about my new status before God!
d. I'm already involved a lot in church work, and I'm not really sure what all the fuss is about.
e. If I'm a minister, then what on earth is the pastor supposed to be doing?
f. I'm glad to know I have my own special calling!
g. Other:

Paul Benjamin puts his finger on a key biblical teaching when he comments,

> . . . responsibility [for church life] is mutually shared. The lack of numerical growth, unmet budgets, or inaccurate announcements become corporate problems, not just individual ones. The congregation asks the question, "What are we going to do about these problems?" (*The Equipping Ministry,* p. 37)

Biblically, we can no longer pass the buck to the pastor. No more can we say, "Hey, pastor, what are you going to do about ____?" If we all are priests, then "you" must become "us" and "he" must become "we."

> A single mother, who belonged to a small group in a church similar to yours, received some tragic news. Her teenage daughter had committed suicide. Unfortunately, this grieving mom had no immediate family or relatives in the area. Her entire small group was quickly notified, and they all took time off from work to minister to her needs. Someone made sure that a group member was with her at all times to offer spiritual and emotional support. Others made all the funeral arrangements, prepared food, ran errands, made phone calls, contacted the school, and took care of the hundred other details that attend such a tragedy. One of the small-group leaders in their church even had the funeral. They wrapped the mother in ongoing love and prayer.
>
> On the day of the daughter's death the church secretary had called the pastor, who was participating in a seminar in another state. "Should I fly back today?" he inquired. "No," the secretary replied, "the church members are meeting her needs just fine." After a worship service three weeks later, the pastor went over to this mother and asked, "How are you doing?" She smiled and answered, "I have never felt so cared for in my life!"

Reflection

In relation to the priesthood of all believers, what is the common thread that runs through the following three Spirit of Prophecy quotes?

1. "God could have committed the message of the gospel, and all the work of loving ministry, to the heavenly angels. He

might have employed other means for accomplishing His purpose. But in His infinite love He chose to make us co-workers with Himself, with Christ and the angels, that we might share the blessings, the joy, the spiritual uplifting, which results from this unselfish ministry." (*Steps to Christ*, p. 79-80)

2. "It is in working for others that they will keep their own souls alive. If they will become colaborers with Jesus, we shall see the light in our churches steadily burning brighter and brighter, sending forth its rays to penetrate the darkness beyond their own borders." (*Historical Sketches*, p. 291)

3. "Ministers may preach pleasing and forcible discourses, and much labor may be put forth to build up and make the church prosperous; but unless its individual members shall act their part as servants of Jesus Christ, the church will ever be in darkness and without strength." (*Testimonies*, vol. 4, p. 285, 286)

Review Questions

1. What difference could it make in your life if you took Peter's revelation in 1 Peter 2:9 seriously? Be specific.

2. If I compared how I feel right now about my role as a minister to a basketball game, I would be. . . . (complete the sentence)
   a. not sure I'm on the team
   b. sitting on the bench
   c. needing to go to basketball camp
   d. on the injured list
   e. needing a time out
   f. giving it all I've got

3. If all church members are priests and ministers, should they have an ordination ceremony? How should it compare to that for the pastor?

4. Do you see any difference in importance between the biblical doctrine of baptism by immersion and the doctrine of the priesthood of all believers? Why do you think we emphasize one but not the other?

Love in Action

My Choice:

Give three hugs every day this week.

Your Choice:

Learning to be a Group: It is better to speak for yourself, not others. Use words like "I" and "Me" rather than "You" and "We." Also, go easy on the "oughts" and "shoulds."

Love in Action Feedback: How did the Hug-A-Thon go this past week?

Ice Breaker: Guess Who?

Hey, Pastor!

It doesn't take long before a pastor in a new district hears the familiar words:

"Hey, pastor, have you visited my cousin Bertha and asked her about Jesus yet?"
"Hey, pastor, have you finished running off the bulletin?"
"Hey, pastor, have you visited the Joneses? They haven't been to church in three weeks."
"Hey, pastor, have you figured out how to raise the money we need to fix the piano?"
"Hey, pastor, have you visited with Fred and Alice? I don't think they're getting along too well."
"Hey, pastor, have you planned the Vacation Bible School program yet?"
"Hey, pastor, did you pick up the paint for the primary room?"

The demands on a pastor's time are varied and constant. Many pastors feel they are on call twenty-four hours a day, seven days a week.

> Searing pain stabbed at my lower back as I crouched on the floor of our upstairs master bedroom. Earlier that morning the doctors had inadvertently injected too much dye in my kidneys during one of a series of tests on my rumbling innards. Now, six hours later, the local anesthetic had worn off, and my kidneys were reacting with a vengeance. My wife raced to the pharmacy for a blessed bottle of doctor-prescribed Tylenol to end the misery. As the young(ish) pastor of a two-church district, I had been under increasing strain for many months. I now added to my inner turmoil these unexpected questions about my physical health. In a few days the physician reported that the results from my tests were, thankfully, absolutely normal. "What's wrong with me then?" I asked. "Why the stomach aches, chest pain, headaches, nausea?" "Well," he replied, "my best guess is stress. You'd better make some changes in your lifestyle or this stress could eat you up." I got the message, big time! The next several weeks were devoted to taking a personal inventory. Without question, one of the biggest stressors I identified was the jungle of expectations I tried to hack through every day. As a melancholy "people pleaser," I felt caught between the varied and often conflicting expectations of my Maker, my family, my church members, my employer, and myself.

One church surveyed its members and asked the following question: "How many hours each week do you feel the pastor ought to spend in the following areas?" Then they listed nine or ten specific areas of ministry. When the questionnaires were tallied and the hours for each activity averaged out, the pastor would have had to work about one hundred and twenty hours each week to do everything the members expected.

Sometimes pastors feel pulled in a thousand directions and wind up like the proverbial "jack of all trades." Inevitably questions arise in a pastor's mind: "Who am I?" "Biblically, what am I supposed to be doing?" "Where does God want me to focus my energies the most?"

Many people feel we are fortunate that different pastors fulfill different roles. One pastor, for instance, is a strong visitor, and he does "his thing" in a church district for four or five years. Then the district gets another pastor who is a strong preacher. Next comes a strong administrator. Then arrives a good counselor. Then a great soul winner. Then an expert builder. Then a wonderful fund raiser. Then a marvelous youth worker. Then we're back to a good visitor. And round and round we go until "all the bases are covered over time." This concept may at first seem useful, but it has several severe problems.

First, it encourages a relatively short stay in any one district. It is unheard of within Adventism for a pastor to stay fourteen or fifteen years in the same area. Why? We are not clear as to what the pastor's true job description really is, so it takes a wide variety of pastoral talents to meet the members' expectations.

Second, this "different pastors, different roles" concept fosters the impression that the pastor is the primary minister and problem solver in the church. Rather than using the wide variety of talents among members, we expect that, over time, those talents will be available in several different pastors.

Third, this concept prevents members from forming a close bond with their pastor, in which they, like two marriage partners, learn how to set goals, make plans, and work through problems together. The pastor feels he will be in a district only a short time, so he tends to use programs he is familiar with. When he has done about all the good he knows how to do, he figures it's time to move on. The members are not inclined to get too enthused about any new initiative or ministry the pastor may be fostering because they know he will soon leave, and the new pastor may have an entirely different emphasis. To avoid the disappointment that comes with shifting priorities, the members eventually sit back and say, "What's the point in getting excited since this won't last long anyway?"

Fourth, this concept ignores the truth that, biblically, pastors are specialists. It seems obvious that a teacher ought to have the gift of teaching and a musician ought to have the gift of music. But somehow we feel that most anyone can be a good pastor as long as he is sincere. Pastors do, however, have a specific, biblical job description. Just because most churches over the years have chosen to ignore it doesn't make it any less important.

Reflection

> Studies from many denominations indicate that a pastor's most effective years in a church district usually begin at year seven. For Adventist pastors, the average stay in any one district is well below four years. From your own experience, how can such frequent pastoral moves influence the pastor's effectiveness and the morale of church members?

Clearly understanding the role of the pastor is vital to the health of all churches. But what exactly is this role? Is there any guidance in Scripture? The answer is a resounding Yes. Let's discover the answer together.

One of the best places for understanding the role of the pastor is the book of Ephesians. The Apostle Paul wrote this book late in his ministry while imprisoned in Rome. Many feel it represents his greatest, most lofty thinking regarding the church. Let's follow Paul's thinking, step by step, as he leads up to the pastor's biblical job description.

God's Plan and Purpose:
Before Paul talks about the pastor himself, he gives us the big picture. Before he focuses our attention on a few puzzle pieces, he wants to show us the picture on the front of the box.

In the first chapter of Ephesians he focuses on the incredible work of the Trinity on our behalf and sums up Their activity by saying,

- The Father has chosen us (verse 4)
- the Son has redeemed us (verse 7)
- the Spirit has sealed us (verse 13)

Paul then gets to the heart of the matter by unveiling what the Trinity is trying to accomplish with all this heavenly activity and sacrifice. In Ephesians 1:10, he writes, "That . . . He might gather together in one all things in Christ, both which are in heaven, and which are on earth, even in Him."

Here is the Godhead's overall plan for Their creation. Heaven's ceaseless activity, unremitting attention, and incredible sacrifice have a very special purpose—*oneness in Christ*. In a world that is full of strife, fractured relationships, blame, criticism, loneliness, and independence, the Trinity is working twenty-four hours a day to bring people together. This plan even includes heavenly beings "which are in heaven." The onlooking universe is drawn closer to God as they see His grace at work in the lives of sinners.

Author Homer Kent has observed:

> Paul, therefore, is stating that now God has revealed to us His plan for the management of the universe. It consists in bringing together all things in Christ. This includes "all things," both in heaven and on earth. (*Ephesians: The Glory of the Church,* p. 24)

The Trinity is trying to establish the unity and wholeness that was tragically demolished by sin. From racial discrimination to shattered families, from financial oppression to gang wars, the Godhead is trying desperately to heal broken lives and unite people in love.

Paul then shares a stirring truth: The Godhead's plan for the entire universe is to be accomplished primarily through the church! "That through the church the manifold wisdom of God might now be made known. . . . This was according to the eternal purpose which he has realized in Christ Jesus our Lord . . ." (Ephesians 3:10 RSV).

The church produces oneness in others by revealing the "wisdom of God." The church creates oneness in the universe by living God's love, by revealing the "fullness of Him [Christ] that filleth all in all" (Ephesians 1:22-23). Created beings are drawn together as they are drawn to the God the church reveals.

Throughout Ephesians Paul refers to the church as a potentially dynamic source of unity and oneness in a broken world:

- But now in Christ Jesus ye who sometimes were far off are made nigh (2:13)

- And that he might reconcile both unto God in one body (2:16)
- In whom ye also are *builded together* (2:22)
- Endeavoring to keep the *unity of the Spirit* (4:3)

Jesus gave this remarkable plan for oneness great emphasis in His stirring prayer in John 17:

- that they may be *one,* as we are (verse 11)
- that they all may be *one;* as thou, Father, art in me, and I in thee, that they also may be *one* in us: that the world may believe that thou hast sent me" (verse 21)
- the glory which thou gavest me I have given them; that they may be *one,* even as we are one (verse 22)
- I in them, and thou in me, that they may be made perfect in *one* (verse 23)

God's plan for putting an end to mistrust, strife, and torn relationships is to be accomplished primarily through the church. The church is to be a special place of healing and wholeness. God wants your church to be known as the "love and unity center" of your community. How tragic it is then for members to quarrel or point fingers at each other. All too often churches do not have a clear understanding of their biblical destiny and therefore fall far short of the mark.

Reflection

In what ways does your life feel most fractured these days? What could help bring you more of a sense of unity and wholeness?

God's Method for Accomplishing His Plan:

In chapter 4 of Ephesians Paul talks about God's method for achieving oneness in and through the church. Here Paul also begins to zero in on the work of the pastor.

Paul lists God's three practical steps for making this Godlike unity a reality:

1. In Ephesians 4:7 Paul says that Christ gave spiritual gifts to His church. There are more than twenty of these gifts and abilities available from the Spirit. These spiritual gifts are listed in more detail in the books of Romans and Corinthians. (Read Romans 12:4-8 and 1 Corinthians 12:27-31.)

2. Next, Paul tells us in Ephesians 4:12 why these spiritual gifts were given to members:
   (a) "for the work of ministry"—loving service to others, and
   (b) "the building up of the body of Christ"—inner spiritual growth.

   Spiritual gifts are far more than another tool to get people busy in church. In Ephesians 4:13, Paul expresses his ultimate desire that the church grow into "the measure of the stature of the fulness of Christ."

   The first two parts, then, of God's unity strategy are to (1) give spiritual gifts to His people that enable them to (2) express God's loving care to those around them and thus grow into maturity in Christ.

   Those very ministries of love fulfill the Godhead's purpose in an incredible variety of ways. The

Christian homemaker, the parent, the lawyer, the secretary, the plumber, the teacher, the banker, and so on, can all become part of God's healing purpose as they touch lives in our sin-infected world.

3. Third, God's plan calls for certain people to specialize in making sure that other people are able to open and use their gifts properly. In Ephesians 4:11-12 Paul tells us about four unique gifts that were given for the express purpose of activating, developing, and coordinating the other spiritual gifts. These gifts are:
    - Apostles
    - Prophets
    - Evangelists
    - Pastors/Teachers (this is a dual gift, not two separate gifts)

   In 4:12 Paul says that these four gifts were given, "For the equipping of the saints."

   One biblical meaning of the word equip is to "mend nets" (Matthew 4:21). It has to do with "the bringing of the saints to a condition of fitness for the discharge of their functions in the Body" (*The Epistle of Paul to the Ephesians*, p. 120). Equipping carries the idea of
    - mending church members
    - fitting them
    - teaching them
    - molding and
    - training them
    - to utilize their God-given gifts and talents.

   So what, then, is the role of the pastor? According to Ephesians his primary responsibility is to equip members to become mature Christians who use their spiritual gifts to minister Jesus' love both in the church and in the world.

In a very real sense the pastor is like a coach or orchestra conductor. He is responsible for making sure that all the spiritual gifts function effectively together. Would you think a coach was effective if you saw him carrying the ball down the field by himself? Isn't his success measured by the ability to make winners out of others?

Note this emphasis by Kenneth Van Wyk:

> Thus we see that the [church] is made up of pastors who do the training and the rest of the laity who carry out the ministry. This clearly is a reversal of the traditionally accepted roles. Therefore, a re-education process is necessary. . . . (*The Caring System,* p. 91)

Reflection

When I think of my pastor following the biblical model and becoming an equipper, I feel: (choose one and indicate why)

a. Concerned
b. Hopeful
c. Excited
d. Upset
e. Confused

For further insight, read carefully and prayerfully the following quotes from the Spirit of Prophecy on the work of the pastor:

> In some respects the pastor occupies a position similar to that of the foreman of a gang of laboring men or the captain of a ship's crew. They are expected to see that the men over whom they are set, do the work assigned to them correctly and promptly, and only in case of emergency are they to execute in detail. The owner of a large mill once found his superintendent in a wheel-pit, making some simple repairs, while a half-dozen workmen in that line were standing by, idly looking on. The proprietor, after learning the facts, so as to be sure that no injustice was done, called the foreman to his office and handed him his discharge with full pay.
>
> In surprise the foreman asked for an explanation. It was given in these words: "I employed you to keep six men at work. I found the six idle, and you doing the work of but one. Your work could have been done just as well by any one of the six. I cannot afford to pay the wages of seven for you to teach the six how to be idle." If pastors would give more attention to getting and keeping their flock actively engaged at work, they would accomplish more good, have more time for study and religious visiting and also avoid many causes of friction. (*Gospel Workers,* p. 197, 198)
>
> Those who have the spiritual oversight of the church should devise ways and means by which an opportunity may be given to every member of the church to act some part in God's work. Too often in the past this has not been done. Plans have not been clearly laid and fully carried out whereby the talents of all might be employed in active service. There are but few who realize how much has been lost because of this. (*Testimonies,* vol. 9, p. 116)
>
> Ministers should not do the work which belongs to the church, thus wearying themselves, and preventing others from performing their duty. They should teach the members how to labor in the church and in the community. (*Historical Sketches,* p. 291)

The Spirit of Prophecy clearly casts the pastor in the role of overseer, trainer, and coach. He is supposed to minister *through* the members, not *instead of* them.

> Imagine a terrible earthquake where more than ten thousand people are injured and dying in a remote area of northern India. As the only physician nearby, Dr. John is called in to help. Within two hours the helicopter puts him down in the midst of appalling carnage and human suffering. As far as the eye can see people are strewn across the landscape crying out in pain from fractures, lacerations, and dreadful internal injuries. Medical facilities are nonexistent. What should he do? What is the best strategy for ministering to such overwhelming need? Dr. John looks for the most critically injured in the vast assemblage and begins to personally minister to their needs. He focuses his attention on the weakest, the most deeply wounded. Even though he works as hard as he can, the doctor is nonetheless able to meet the needs of relatively few. While he provides medical assistance to those about him, hundreds and thousands of others are left unattended. Many die in misery. After three days of constant effort, Dr. John's own energies and meager resources are completely exhausted.
>
> Picture now a different scenario. Dr. Andrew is flown into the same disaster. He, however, adopts a dramatically different strategy. First, Andrew looks around for the strongest in the crowd, those who are wounded the least. Even though hundreds are crying out in pain for his assistance, he focuses instead on identifying those he can quickly train and mobilize to help. Some are sent in search of water, food, and blankets. Others are organized to make bandages and set up a transportation network. Dr. Andrew selects a dozen of those with only minor wounds to watch as he himself works on several bleeding patients. After learning the rudiments of first aid, these twelve students are sent out to train still others. Eventually scores of teams are created that scatter across the countryside ministering to an ever widening circle of need. (Adapted from Carl George, *How To Break Growth Barriers,* p. 13)

The difference between Dr. John and Dr. Andrew is the fundamental choice faced by pastors and churches today. Will the pastor focus on doing the ministry himself or on equipping others? Many pastors spend the majority of their time, like Dr. John, ministering spiritually to the neediest in their congregation. Such a pastor spends his day personally helping those with the deepest wounds, the most critical spiritual patients. After all, isn't that what we pay him to do? He is living the traditional "shepherd" role that most Adventists today have come to expect. The problem is that such a scenario is unbiblical. In essence, such pastors are doing the members' ministry for them. Because of cultural pressures, the expectations of others, and the pastor's own desire to help, churches can get locked into a cycle that is out of harmony with Scripture.

Instead of focusing on the weakest, pastors should be primarily targeting the strongest, as did Dr. Andrew. To fulfill their role as equippers, pastors need to spend the majority of their time with that segment of the congregation that is the healthiest spiritually and emotionally, training them to minister. Pastors should mentor the most mature Christians in order to multiply themselves and build ministry leaders who can, in turn, equip others. The goal is to develop an ever-expanding base of caregivers who can meet far more needs than one person ever could alone. The direct ministry these pastors do provide to hurting people will primarily be for the purpose of training others. Notice how Jesus modeled such an approach: "In all His work He was training [the disciples] for individual labor. . ." (*Acts of the Apostles*, p. 32).

It is a real eye-opener to realize that whenever Jesus ministered to those in need, His primary purpose was always to teach His disciples. In that sense He was like a player/coach. The New Testament church was built upon Jesus' ingenious strategy of pouring Himself primarily into just a dozen disciples, who then discipled others. He built leaders who built others. When pastors spend most of their time dispensing spiritual first aid alone, no matter how legitimate the needs, they are ultimately weakening the congregation as a whole. The pastor's calling is to make provision for the needs not just of the people on the Adventist church books, but for all the wounded throughout the community. Only Dr. Andrew's strategy can accomplish that. Congregations must intentionally choose what direction they want their pastor to pursue—tradition or Scripture. Many churches need to enable their pastors to do the opposite of what has been expected in the past.

Reflection

Which physician in the above story appears more caring at first, Dr. John or Dr. Andrew? Which one is ultimately more caring? If you were hurting, would you accept the ministry of a fellow church member as equal to that of the pastor?

After hearing his pastor teach these truths, one church member remarked, "Hey, I know what our pastor is really trying to do. He's trying to get out of work! Man, if we do ministry, what's he going to do all day—sit at home sipping lemonade and daydreaming?" This person needed to have his eyes opened. When your pastor steps into his biblical role as coach, he will not be working less, he will be working smarter. A coach's work is different from that of the players, but it is no less arduous. In fact, it is usually the coach who stays after practice working alone to develop new plays and strategies. Only the coach carries the well-being of all the players on his heart. Anyone who has been involved in training others knows well that it is much easier to "do it yourself." As a coach, your pastor will do far more than simply train people for ministry. He will be building people. He will be equipping them to become mature, loving, balanced disciples. That is some of the hardest, most challenging work ever entrusted to humans.

The point here is not for a pastor to dump his legitimate work on the church members. The pastor should enable the members to find their own God-given gifts and ministries. If he is currently doing their ministry for them, he must give it back.

When one pastor saw these truths he made the following confession:

> I still remember the day when I had to get out of my chair in my office and fall flat on my face on the rug, asking God to forgive me, because He had shown me clearly that I would be held responsible for every ministry I stole from my people. And I had a list of them. I asked God to show me how to avoid that in the future. (*Love, Acceptance and Forgiveness,* J. Cook-Regal, p. 60)

Reflection

The following is a list of some of the responsibilities of a certain pastor. Place an "X" by those functions you feel this pastor should stop doing and delegate so that he can spend more time on his true biblical role as an equipper.

- ☐ Prepare the weekly church bulletin
- ☐ Give Bible studies
- ☐ Conduct health seminars for the community
- ☐ Visit the sick in the local hospital
- ☐ Lead out in Ingathering
- ☐ Oversee the fund raising campaign for remodeling the church
- ☐ Organize the housing for a visiting singing group
- ☐ Help organize Vacation Bible School
- ☐ Attend the finance committee meetings
- ☐ Conduct a small group
- ☐ Attend the deacons' and deaconesses' meetings
- ☐ Attend the Sabbath school council meetings
- ☐ Spend time teaching leaders how to lead
- ☐ Attend the school committee meetings
- ☐ Attend the elders' meetings
- ☐ Attend the youth council meetings
- ☐ Chair the local church board meetings
- ☐ Lead out in prayer meeting
- ☐ Find a new teacher for the primary division
- ☐ Counsel church members who are having marital difficulties
- ☐ Visit inactive members
- ☐ Visit shut-ins regularly
- ☐ Deal with disruptive church members who hold extreme views
- ☐ Take time each day to study how to be an equipper
- ☐ Arrange for special music on Sabbath
- ☐ Get estimates on a new furnace for the church

Now look back over the list above and ask yourself if the choices you made were based on your own personal preferences or on clear biblical teachings. Explain.

The wonderful task that God has assigned to the church will require effective leadership and extraordinary cooperation within the body of Christ. Every pastor I have ever met is human and, therefore, has strengths and weaknesses. It is vital that churches find ways to open up safe, affirming, channels of communication whereby pastors and members alike can honestly dialogue about mutual expectations. The pastoral job description in Ephesians is not a recipe for lockstep conformity. Creativity and individuality are a must. Nonetheless, Paul's vision is clear. Scripture calls pastors to use their talents to equip God's people to become true priests. It also calls members to stop treating the pastor as a "hired hand" who does their ministry for them. The Trinity is counting on each of us to make the right choice so that God's plan, as outlined by Paul, can at last be realized.

Review Questions

1. Many pastors stop trying to "give ministry back to the members" because added misunderstanding and frustration can be created in the process. How can your own pastor find enough emotional support in your church to fully implement his true biblical role as coach?

2. How would you answer this concern?
   "I can see that God has a 'grand design' for His church, but frankly I often struggle just to get through the day! How can meeting deadlines at work, raising two pesky teenagers, and doing dishes possibly fit into some grand purpose? I'm just trying to survive!"

3. I feel the best way to begin cooperating with God's plan is: (circle all that apply)
   a. For me to study these topics further myself
   b. For me to discuss these things personally with my pastor
   c. For our local church leaders to study these topics together
   d. For me to change my own attitudes and expectations
   e. For our Body Building Group to educate others and support change
   f. Other:

Love in Action—Important!

My Choice:

Put your loose change in a jar every day for a week and bring the jar to the next group meeting when you study "High-Rise Christians." At that meeting assign two members to think of a present they can buy for a person who is hurting.

Your Choice:

Learning to be a Group: Effective groups focus not only on learning, but also on building relationships. How we treat each other as we learn is as important as the learning itself. Effective groups also serve others. Ice Breakers, Group Activities, and Love in Action are important because they help bring balance to group life.

Love in Action Feedback: Time to put all the jar money into one pile. Assign two people to buy a present and deliver it this week to someone who is hurting.

Group Activity: Know Your String Bean.

High-Rise Christians

In this lesson we begin looking at the vital topic of spiritual gifts more carefully. Spiritual gifts are designed to build high-rise Christians.

> Have you ever watched a high-rise being built? On my way to college classes in Boston years ago, I watched construction crews spend months building a massive foundation—clearing, digging, drilling test holes, making sure steel pylons were pounded down to bedrock, laying out plumbing, setting up forms, pouring cement, and on and on. Week after tiring week. The uninformed passersby might think all of this is a waste of time. "Shouldn't they be building up, not down?" they might say. But the higher the building, the more important the foundation.
>
> The famous 110-story Sears Tower in Chicago reaches 1,454 stomach-churning feet into the sky and weighs 445 million pounds. That magnificent structure is supported by 114 pillars buried in the foundation. Each pillar is sunk as deep in the earth as the Statue of Liberty is tall. The foundation took months to build, but there would be no tower without it.

To begin by jumping into a definition of each spiritual gift might satisfy many people's curiosity, but it would be like starting to build on the eighth story with no foundation. Some things cannot be rushed. You may grow radishes in thirty days, but not oak trees. When it comes to building and growing people, Adventists should be in the high-rise and oak tree business. We have too many shacks and radishes already! In this lesson we will put in place several foundation stones that help us understand God's purpose in giving us spiritual gifts.

Foundation Block #1: Spiritual gifts teach us about our worth.
One of the most fundamental sources of emotional difficulty for thousands of people is the epidemic of low self-esteem that is rampant throughout the United States today. Church members are not immune. People who suffer from low self-esteem often deal with it inappropriately by either throwing off all ethical restraints or by adhering outwardly to a rigid system of rules and regulations. The first group feels they are worthless anyway, "so why try?" The other class tries to earn acceptance by strictly conforming to other people's expectations. Over the years the Seventh-day Adventist church's admirably high standards have attracted this latter class in droves. Eventually, however, the rules alone do not satisfy. As a result, many of our pews are populated by members who are complying on the outside but dying on the inside. They are caught in a "no man's land" of spiritual insecurity. A big part of the remedy is for them to sense their infinite value before God.

They need to hear the wonderful truth about God's unconditional love. They need to hear that God never sees crowds, only individuals. They need to hear that God loves them as if they were the only individuals in His entire universe. He is even more interested in their happiness than they are. "One soul is of such value that, in comparison with it, worlds sink into insignificance . . ." (*Desire of Ages*, p. 561).

We are so special to God that He knows each of us by name. "But now thus saith the Lord that created thee . . . Fear not: for I have redeemed thee, I have called thee by thy name; thou art mine" (Isaiah 43:1).

That's very important to me because people I meet get my first name messed up most of the time. I even get mail addressed to "Miss" Kim Johnson. (Imagine how it feels for a guy to be sent sample perfume in a frilly box or invitations to attend the next seminar on "Stress Secrets for Women.") When Christ greets me at the Second Coming, He is not going to say, "Hi, what's-your-face." He's not going to be like most people and call me Tim or Jim. He will say, "Kim! Kim Allan Johnson, I'm thrilled that you're here." He knows me.

In the three parables of lost things in Luke 15, Jesus emphasizes the value of one person. He doesn't say "several" sheep were searched for, or a "bunch" of coins, or a "group" of brothers. It was just one.

Christians need to be reminded often that Christ would have died for them alone.

> Imagine a large retinue of angels nearing the Holy City in heaven on the return journey from earth after the Second Coming. A million-voice angel choir within the city strikes a glorious, heart-pounding chorus. They have been practicing for this moment for centuries. Another million representatives from unfallen worlds are there to greet the redeemed. The miles-long table, laden with heavenly dishes for the victory dinner, is ready. The atmosphere is electric. Finally the huge front gate of the city is thrown open to let in the redeemed. Occupants of the Holy City line the tops of the walls. All eyes strain for a glimpse of the saved. The angelic escort from earth nears—and the only one saved is you! Out of earth's billions, you are the only one who accepted Christ as Saviour. From all the effort and sacrifice heaven has expended, you are the only fruit. Everyone is stunned into silence. Then Jesus steps forward, puts His powerful and tender arms around you, and gives you a big bear hug just as He did at the Second Coming. He turns to the onwatching throng, then back to you, and declares with tears of joy in His voice, "You are worth it all!"

Our insecure members need to hear that truth over and over.

It is that same message of value and importance that is inherent in the doctrine of spiritual gifts. God gave you gifts because He wants you. The Apostle Paul compares you and your spiritual gifts to the parts of the human body, then tells us that "God has arranged the parts in the body, every one of them, just as He wanted them to be" (1 Corinthians 12:18 NIV).

You have been chosen, specially placed, and gifted. You are equipped through your spiritual gifts to fulfill a unique, indispensable role in the Kingdom of God. You are irreplaceable. Your particular mixture of gifts, personality, and experience are unique in the universe. Others may do something similar, but never the same. You can help certain people in a way no one else can. You can love like no one else. You are as unique as your fingerprints, and God has a place in His plan for you.

Reflection

A friend confides in you that he has read all the Bible verses about self-worth and still feels like a "weed in God's garden." What can help?

Foundation Block #2: Spiritual gifts give us a sense of belonging.
In order to reach their fullest potential and discover lasting joy, humans desperately need to sense that they belong. Individuals may be so scarred and numbed by life experiences that they actually feel safer in solitude. But deep inside, even these people need to belong to someone or some group in order to be whole. That yearning may be reduced to a faint whisper, but it is there. In the first half of this century the extended family provided an invaluable place of belonging. Neighbors visited. Communities were close-knit. But that has changed. People are crying out, searching, knowing that something is missing. Churches are not exempt. One man sadly described church as a place where we come to be lonely together. You can be lonely in a crowd.

Spiritual gifts were designed by God to put people on the fast track to belonging. Suppose I am gifted by God to be a foot in the body of Christ. As wonderful as feet are, they were not designed to function alone. They need to be attached to a leg, which is attached to a hip, which is attached to a torso. The doctrine of spiritual gifts shouts at us—"You need each other, you all belong together!" The Apostle Paul put it this way,

> Now the body is not made up of one part but of many. If the foot should say, "Because I am not a hand, I do not belong to the body," it would not for that reason cease to be part of the body. (1 Corinthians 12:14-15 NIV)

God wants us on His team. The position we will play is determined by our spiritual gifts. In elementary school I hated recess because I was always chosen last. Being small for my age, I often heard those stinging words, "Oh, teacher, do we have to pick Johnson?" I was on the team, but I never felt wanted. As a Christian, that is all different. As God looks over at the crowd, He sees me shuffling my feet and looking nervously at the ground. He comes over, puts His large, calloused hand on my shoulder, and says, "Kim, you're just who I've been looking for. You've got the spiritual gifts required to get the job done. Would you please be on My team?" Wow, would I ever! I belong.

Reflection

Can you think of a time in your life when you were genuinely accepted into a team or group that was important to you? What was that like?

Foundation Block #3: Spiritual gifts teach us that we all have a spiritual calling.
We need to recover the New Testament sense of spiritual vocation or calling. Your spiritual gifts are not some tool you use only when doing "church work." They are as much a part of you as the ability to speak. They are an integral part of you at home, church, and in the community. You see, your real full-time work is being a minister. That is your full-time calling in whatever sphere you find yourself.

Writing in the context of spiritual gifts, the Apostle Paul counsels the church members at Ephesus, "I urge you to live a life worthy of the calling you have received" (Ephesians 4:1 NIV). All are called of God, just as much as the pastor.

> When I was pastoring years ago, a church member commented resignedly, "I sure wish I could be called to the ministry full time like you. But I'm just a plumber." I responded, "I must apologize to you. I must have done an awful job of explaining who you are as a Christian. You have a full-time spiritual calling just as I do. When you were baptized you received spiritual gifts to equip you for that calling. You and I just happen to minister in different ways. You see, a pastor's ministry is focused largely toward church members. If someone is called by God to be a full-time mother, then her ministry will be mostly at home. If someone works as a janitor, teacher, technician, mechanic, physician, or real estate agent, then that person's ministry is largely expressed through that particular responsibility. In fact, as a plumber, you have a very vital ministry because you rub shoulders with non-Christians all day. As pastor, I only see non-Christians part of the time."

According to the Apostle Paul, you and the pastor are both "body parts" (1 Corinthians 12:12). We are one whole, each doing our God-given parts to serve the Head, Jesus Christ. The entire human body exists to serve the brain. If the brain wants to go somewhere, God gave us legs and feet to take it there. If the brain wants to read a book, God gave us eyes for the brain to see. If the brain needs food and water to function, then God gave us a mouth and a stomach to drink and eat. Likewise, the heart does not have a more exalted calling than the stomach or pancreas. The foot does not have a higher calling than the liver or vocal chords. In the same way, we are all called to serve the Head, Jesus, in *all* we do.

Part of our problem is that we get all messed up in defining "sacred" and "secular." You do not go to your "secular job" and then do some witnessing on Sabbath afternoon. We somehow think pastoring is sacred, while accounting and construction are secular. When you accept Christ, all that you do becomes an act of worship. Being a secretary or janitor can be a holy calling.

So what is the difference between sacred and secular anyway? God called the ground Moses stood on "holy." It was the same dirt as before. It looked just like all the dirt around it. The difference was the *presence of God.* That's what makes something sacred. When God lives in us through His Spirit, then whatever the Spirit guides us to do becomes a sacred endeavor.

Sacred also has to do with the *purpose* for which something is used. Things can be good or bad depending on their purpose. A knife can be used to do surgery or rob a market. Grape juice can be a refreshing drink or be allowed to ferment and produce drunk drivers. Money can be used to gamble or buy medicine. The seven days of the week were all alike until God singled out the seventh for a special spiritual purpose. Moses' rod was just another stick until God told him to use it to accomplish His will. Likewise, our work in the home and community is just like everyone else's until our hearts are given to God. At that very moment those same jobs become sacred responsibilities. They take on a spiritual purpose and are used by God to reveal His character of love, excellence, justice, and mercy. They become a means of glorifying Him.

God never designed that our lives should be sectioned into "sacred" and "secular." That is an artificial, Western distinction. For the Christian, if we sense our high calling, all we touch will have the glory of God in view. Spiritual gifts, then, are designed to operate in the broadest possible sphere. Even the natural talents you were born with, when dedicated to God, become part of your sacred calling. God wants to use all your talents, abilities, hobbies, personality, and experience.

Notice how the Spirit of Prophecy applies this concept to the life of Christ:

> The greater part of our Saviour's life on earth was spent in patient toil in the carpenter's shop at Nazareth. . . . He was as faithfully fulfilling His mission while working at His humble trade as when He healed the sick or walked upon the storm-tossed waves of Galilee. So in the humblest duties and lowliest positions of life, we may walk and work with Jesus. (*Steps to Christ,* p. 81)

When you prepare to start work in the morning, don't forget to put on your priestly robes. You are a minister to your world, whatever it is.

Reflection

Someone has said that even peeling potatoes can be a sacred endeavor. How can that be?

Foundation Block #4: Spiritual gifts free us from guilt placed on us by others.
As we understand our calling and identify our ministries, the doctrine of spiritual gifts can eliminate a lot of unnecessary guilt and burnout. You do not have all the gifts of the Spirit and are held accountable only for what God has given you. Too often well-meaning nominating committees use guilt to get people to take on responsibilities in the church. The doctrine of spiritual gifts frees you to say No to without feeling guilty. You may choose to fill in during an emergency, but God only holds you responsible for using what He has given. If your gifts are oriented toward working behind the scenes, you should not feel guilty about not being up front. If your gift is hospitality and making new people feel welcome in the church, you should not feel guilty about not going door to door handing out literature. If your gift is administration, you should not feel guilty about not conducting a Revelation Seminar.

The Apostle Paul teaches, "If the whole body were an eye, where would the sense of hearing be? If the whole body were an ear, where would the sense of smell be?" (1 Corinthians 12:17 NIV). We are not supposed to force all members into one or two molds. One size does not fit all.

You are responsible for finding your own God-given ministry under the guidance and oversight of your local church. When you find that particular place in God's plan, it should be fulfilling and joyful. It is man, not God, who gives people burdens too heavy to bear.

Reflection

What is the easiest way to get you to accept responsibilities you don't want? What most often keeps you from saying No to people's unrealistic demands on your time?

Foundation Block #5: Spiritual gifts enable God to continue the Incarnation.
The work of Christ in loving humanity to Himself was accomplished through incarnation. He became Man so that we could see His broad smile, feel His warm embrace, hear His words of hope, and watch Him bleed. In Acts 1:1, Luke says he recounted "all that Jesus *began* both to do and teach." According to Luke, Jesus' ministry had only begun after He spent thirty-three years on this earth. From His birth to the ascension, Jesus only had time to get started on what He really wanted to accomplish. How is His ministry to continue? The Apostle Paul teaches plainly, "Now you are the body of Christ and members in particular" (1 Corinthians 12:27). The responsibility has been transferred, and it's time for the second team to take the field. What a responsibility is ours!

But Jesus was so magnificently talented, so immensely caring, so full of wisdom and power. How can anyone adequately represent Him? How can anyone fully recapture His ministry? Good question, but that was never God's plan anyway. Christ is to be represented by the entire body of Christ, the church. That's why we need to work as a team. Collectively we can more nearly approximate the multi-faceted ministry of Jesus. And the way we find out what part of Jesus' body we are supposed to be is by discovering our spiritual gifts. If we do not fulfill our place as a member of the body, then Jesus is handicapped. Can you picture Christ walking on crutches? Can you see Him unable to breathe adequately and having to rest frequently by the side of the road? That's what happens to Him today if the legs and lungs of His church let their spiritual gifts lie dormant.

Notice what important truth the Apostle Peter reveals in 1 Peter 4:10: "As every man hath received the gift, even so minister the same one to another, as good stewards of the manifold grace of God."

The Apostle calls us the stewards, or mangers, of the grace of God. Peter reveals that one of the primary ways in which the God's grace flows out to humanity is through spiritual gifts. God has voluntarily made Himself dependent on us. What a sobering thought.

Reflection

In what ways could your church be at fault in turning formerly active members into spectators?

Foundation Block #6: Using our spiritual gifts is a key to fulfilling our eternal destiny.
God has an incredible plan for our eternal future. At the center of that plan is for us to learn how to be co-workers with Him in this life. In that sense, eternity begins now.

> For we are laborers together with God. (1 Corinthians 3:9)

> One who believes in Jesus Christ as a personal Saviour is to be a co-worker with Him, bound up with His heart of infinite love, cooperating with Him in works of self-denial and benevolence. (Ellen White, *Medical Ministry,* p. 315)

When the disciples followed Christ, each new day was full of surprises. Our own days can be like that if we surrender them to God and pray, "Lord use my spiritual gifts and talents today to your glory. Bring into my life the people You want me to help. Put me in the situations with You that You desire." Then turn the radar on and expect God to be active in and through your routine. He will surely send you people who need a hug, a smile, a word of encouragement, guidance, or a listening ear.

This life, however, is just a training ground for the ministry God has planned for each of us in the earth made new. This little life is a brief internship for the world to come. We develop here the rudiments of a partnership with God that will take on unimaginable dimensions in the hereafter. As illustrated by Joseph and Daniel in the Old Testament, we will be exalted from this prison house of sin to positions of amazing responsibility and privilege in the New Earth.

The Bible does not give us a lot of specifics on what our future roles will be, but it does provide enough information to fuel our holy imaginations and energize our souls.

First, the Bible indicates that we will be kings:

> Unto Him that loved us . . . and hath made us kings. . . . (Revelation 1:5-6)

> To him that overcometh will I grant to sit with me in my throne. . . . (Revelation 3:21)

Remember Jesus' words to us in the parable of the talents:

> Well done, good and faithful servant; thou hast been faithful over a few things, I will make thee ruler over many things. . . . (Matthew 25:23)

Who can even imagine what "many things" would include? We will apparently have some type of supervisory role in the earth made new. Jesus might say, "Beth, I would like you to oversee the people and planets in the new Lindora System."

Another prospect in the New Earth will be for us to minister in God's presence:

> Therefore are they before the throne of God, and serve him day and night in his temple: and he that sitteth on the throne shall dwell among them. (Revelation 7:15)

> Him that overcometh will I make a pillar in the temple of my God. . . . (Revelation 3:12)

Notice what the *Seventh-day Adventist Bible Commentary* says about the previous verse: "Accordingly, this promise would mean that the overcomer will hold a permanent, important place in the very presence of God" (*Seventh-day Adventist Bible Commentary*, vol. 7, p. 759).

Once sin is eradicated, God will continue His amazing plans for the universe, plans that were temporarily interrupted by sin. And we will be at the center of it all, as God's closest associates—studying, learning, planning, consulting, representing, worshiping, and offering praise. This little earth will be exalted to become headquarters of the universe, and we will be exalted in wide-eyed wonder to a place of mind-boggling privilege and responsibility.

> The privileges of those who overcome by the blood of the Lamb and the word of their testimony are beyond comprehension. (Ellen White, *Maranatha,* p. 367)

> He that used the two talents entrusted in this life, will, in the future life, show that his talents have not been corrupted. They will be used on a wider and nobler plan. . . . (Ellen White, *The Upward Look,* p. 97)

And the essential preparation for all of that glorious future is now, as we use our spiritual gifts in fulfilling our calling here.

Because we have developed such a deep, enduring partnership with God in this life, we will have another special function in eternity. In the New Earth, God will be counting on our testimony of His goodness to keep the universe secure against a second rebellion. Note what the apostle Paul teaches in this regard:

> But God, who is rich in mercy, for his great love wherewith he loved us, even when we were dead in sins hath [made us alive] together with Christ (by grace ye are saved) . . . that in the ages to come he might show the exceeding riches of his grace in his kindness toward us through Christ Jesus. (Ephesians 2:4-7)

Paul says that in the "ages to come" we will be privileged to become Exhibit A of God's love. Our testimony of His goodness will be an essential safeguard against sin rising again. We will not remember the horrors of earth. No tear or sting of sorrow will mar eternity. Nonetheless, you will have a story to tell. The unfallen worlds will gather around you by the billions and hang on your every word. "You were down there? You are one of the saved ones?" No one may seem interested in your spiritual journey here on earth, but the unfallen worlds will treat you as special. As they gather around in the earth made new, what story will you tell? Will it be a story of faith and love? A story of serving others? A story of adventuring for God? Will it be a story of using your spiritual gifts to His glory?

Review Questions

1. Which of the foundation blocks in this lesson meant the most to you and why?

2. What does the phrase "High-Rise Christian" mean to you?

3. This small group can help me be a High-Rise Christian by. . . . (circle all that apply)
   a. Listening without judging
   b. Being open about their own struggles
   c. Taking time to socialize together periodically
   d. Praying for me
   e. Giving me a swift kick in the pants when I need it
   f. Helping me find answers
   g. Cheerleading to help keep me motivated

Learning to be a Group: Be sure to begin and end the meeting on time, except for unusual circumstances. Those who want to share further can be invited to stay by afterwards.

Love in Action Feedback: How did the purchase and delivery of the present work out?

Ice Breaker: What is one of the most memorable gifts you ever received? Why did it mean so much?

The Joy of Gifts

Phone rings. I pick it up. Lady with hyperactive voice answers. "Hello, Mr. Johnson, I'm Myrtle Marblehead, from Great Giveaways. You've just won a series of marvelous gifts for you and your fine family. You like to receive gifts, don't you, Mr. Johnson? [no pause] Of course you do. As a winner in our random sampling of people in your area, you will receive a trip to Florida for two, a full set of golf clubs, a new watch, video camera, microwave oven, lamp, and electric ear cleaner. I know you're excited." I look at my wife and roll my eyes. "These marvelous gifts are worth $4,500, Mr. Johnson. And we are making them available to you today for only $500! That's a huge saving of $4,000, Mr. Johnson! Did I mention that this offer is only good for a couple more minutes? If you'll just give us your credit card number, we'll get the ball rolling so you can start saving that $4,000 right away!" Long pause. "Mr. Johnson?" I reply, "I'm not interested." Myrtle is incredulous. "I'm not interested." Urgent. One time offer! "I'm really not interested." Starts to replay sales pitch. "Good-bye, ma'am." She speaks more rapidly. "Good-bye. ma'am." Myrtle is still chattering on as I hang up. Since when does "gift" mean getting charged 500 bucks?

A friend follows up on a time-share condo offer. All he has to do is show up at the appointed time, listen to the sales pitch, and walk away with a free color television. No strings attached. He shows up, listens quietly, then says, "No thanks. Now, where is my gift?" He has his choice of three televisions. He plugs one in and discovers it has a black-and-white picture. "Hey," he complains, "this isn't a color TV!" "Sure it is," they reply. "The outside is either red, blue, or yellow."

Human gifts aren't always what they seem. Human gifts can disappoint. But not God's. His gifts are the genuine article. He gives because He longs for us to experience lasting joy. This lesson introduces us to a fascinating source of joy—teaming up with the Trinity to minister to others through our God-given spiritual gifts.

In Matthew 25 Jesus talks about what His last-day church will be like. He presents us with a trilogy of three parables that, properly understood, underscore the importance of spiritual gifts. Please take a few minutes to read the following passages:

1. The ten virgins (Matthew 25:1-13)
2. The talents (Matthew 25:14-30)
3. The sheep and the goats (Matthew 25:31-46)

These three parables are intimately related to each other. They flow one into the other like a stream cascading down a mountain gorge. The sequence is as follows:

1. We receive the Holy Spirit (parable of ten virgins)
2. The Spirit gives us gifts/abilities (parable of the talents)
3. Those spiritual gifts are to be used in unselfish ministries of love (parable of sheep and goats)

In these parables the Holy Spirit, like the wise men at Jesus' birth, comes to us bearing what the Scriptures call spiritual gifts. Our reception of these gifts is one of the key elements in being "filled with the Spirit." The parables reveal that the Spirit actually wants to flow *through* us, not *into* us. We are to be more like pipelines than buckets, letting God's love flow through us to others. All attempts at receiving the Spirit by exclusive, monkish attention to prayer, Bible study, and the cleansing of self will ultimately fail unless they go hand in hand with simultaneous Christlike ministry to others.

Reflection

Compare your current understanding of the topic of spiritual gifts to the weather and tell why you chose the answer you did:

a. Sunny and clear
b. Partly sunny
c. Partly cloudy
d. Foggy
e. Overcast and rainy

The Apostle Paul

The Apostle Paul fully endorsed the importance of spiritual gifts. Notice His comments:

> Now concerning spiritual gifts, brethren, *I would not have you ignorant.* (1 Corinthians 12:1)

> So we, being many, are one body in Christ, and every one members one of another. Having then gifts differing according to the grace that is given to us. . . . (Romans 12:5-6)

Adventist Pioneers

In our early days as a denomination, the doctrine of spiritual gifts was a subject of vital interest. The pioneers focused on complete restoration of every gift of the Spirit. They knew that once people accepted the truth regarding all the gifts, they could then far more easily accept the manifestation of one of those gifts, in particular the writings of Ellen White.

Uriah Smith's article in the *Review and Herald* of 1866, "Answers To Objections Against Visions," is a real eye-opener:

> Seventh-day Adventists believe in the gifts of the Spirit. They believe that the varied operations of the Spirit of God, having been once expressly set in the church—1 Corinthians 12, Ephesians 4—were designed to continue therein to the end. To them, the doctrine of spiritual gifts, as set forth in the chapters referred to, is as much a special doctrine of revelation as is the Sabbath, the sanctuary, the state of the dead, or the Second Advent. . . . They can as easily explain away the Sabbath, baptism, and the Lord's Supper, as the doctrine of spiritual gifts, and hence believe that to reject it is to be guilty of error, and that to receive it is essential to the unity of the faith. (*Review and Herald,* June 12, 1866)

Early Adventists put the truth about spiritual gifts on the same level as the Sabbath, the sanctuary, and the Second Coming of Christ. Ellen White wrote:

> There is a need for a variety of gifts in the Lord's work. Read carefully the fourth chapter of Ephesians. The entire chapter is a description of the Lord's manner of working. Every gift is to be acknowledged as essential to the success of the work. (Letter 8, 1899)

> In all the Lord's arrangements, *there is nothing more beautiful* than His plan of giving to men and women a diversity of gifts. (*Evangelism,* p. 98)

Spiritual gifts can be defined as special abilities and talents given by the Holy Spirit to enable each Christian to play an important part in God's plan for loving and saving humanity.

Scripture lists about twenty spiritual gifts. No one person has all the gifts, and every believer has at least one—"The Spirit dividing to every man severally as He will" (1 Corinthians 12:11). You can find great joy in discovering your gifts. "Now I feel like I know where I really fit!" one longtime church member exclaimed after learning her own gift mix. Too many members accept responsibilities for which they are not gifted and then wonder why they don't enjoy them. Perhaps you have been the lucky recipient of one of those infamous nominating committee phone calls:

> "Hey, Mary, this is Dotty. I'm glad I caught you home! [Dotty? Is that the lady with the wart on her nose? And what is that gaggle of voices in the background?] Mary, how are the kids? Do you still have that job at the hairdresser's? [Hairdresser's? I haven't worked there for eight years. Something is brewing. Dotty never called before, and her tone of voice is too syrupy.] Awful weather, isn't it? [Get to the point, Dotty, the loaf is burning.] Mary, I'm here at the nominating committee [Oh no!], and we were just wondering if there is anyway you could be our Sabbath school superintendent this year. [I hate being up front.] It's really no big deal. It won't take hardly anytime at all. [Oh sure, who are you trying to kid?] Your name keeps coming up over and over, and we just feel it is the Lord speaking to our hearts. [Man, she's really bringing in the big guns. Must be desperate. I'm probably the fiftieth person they've asked.] I know you must be so busy with those three kids [two], the new house [we rent], and that hairdressing thing and all. We just think you're perfect for this job. You're so organized and thoughtful. . . ."

If we are going to take seriously the biblical call to "do church" on the basis of spiritual gifts, then we will have to change the way many nominating committees do their work.

Reflection

> Have you ever accepted a church office that you really didn't want? How did it affect your performance and desire to serve again?

In order for church members to find real joy in using their spiritual gifts, they need to understand the following important truths:

1. Spiritual gifts and natural talents.
Every human being enters this world with certain built-in abilities and acquires others over time. These natural talents come from God, just as life comes from the Creator of all things. But natural talents are separate from Paul's description of spiritual gifts. Atheists can be very "talented" individuals. Paul specifically writes that spiritual gifts are given "by the Spirit" (1 Corinthians 12:8). Christians have both natural talents and spiritual gifts; both can be used for the advancement of Christ's kingdom. Ellen White writes,

> The special gifts of the Spirit are not the only talents represented in the parable [of the talents]. It includes all gifts and endowments, whether original or acquired, natural or spiritual. All are to be employed in Christ's service. (*Christ's Object Lessons,* p. 328)

Reflection

> Are your abilities being used effectively in the church? Would you describe yourself as feeling fulfilled, manipulated, frustrated, or left out? Why?

---

2. Spiritual gifts and the fruit of the Spirit.
Spiritual gifts are not the same as the fruit of the Spirit, which is listed in Galatians 5:22-23—love, joy, peace, long-suffering, gentleness, goodness, faith, meekness, temperance. The fruit deals mostly with who we are and our motives, while the gifts deal mostly with what we do. The Spirit of Prophecy counsels, "God's glory must be the motive of all who are laborers together with Him" (*Christ's Object Lessons*, p. 350).

Sometimes gifts and fruit get separated, with tragic results. For example, the Corinthian church of Paul's day was a pretty pathetic situation. In 1 Corinthians 3:3 Paul writes, "For you are yet carnal, for whereas there is among you envying, strife, and divisions." Later, in 1 Corinthians 11, Paul goes on to describe the Corinthians' unique communion service: "For in eating, every one takes before the other his own supper and one is hungry and another is drunken." They held a communion meal and jealously ate their own goodies, while others who had nothing stood around drooling and holding their stomachs to quiet the hunger pangs. Others took the occasion to get drunk.

The Corinthian church was not without spiritual gifts (see chapter 14), but they were desperately lacking in love. Paul hits the nail squarely on the head when he says,

> And though I have the [spiritual] gift of prophecy, and understand all mysteries and all knowledge, and though I have faith so that I could remove mountains, and have not love, I am nothing. (1 Corinthians 13:2)

I have often told nominating committees, "If you really want to see if someone is fit to fill a church office or not, just replace the person and see how he reacts." We all serve at the discretion of the body. We are servants, not power brokers. Service is a privilege, not a right. If people get bent out of shape when they are replaced, that is proof that they were never fit to fill that office in the first place.

3. Gifts and Roles
There is often confusion between spiritual gifts and what are called "Christian roles." For instance, every Christian has the privilege of communing with God in prayer. That is one of our "roles." But someone with the spiritual gift of Intercessory Prayer will make prayer a ministry. They enjoy spending unusual amounts of time in

prayer and feel a passion to pray for others. Another example is hospitality. All Christians should be hospitable, but someone with that spiritual gift will exercise hospitality with much more ease, effectiveness, and joy. Every Christian also has the role of a witness, but not everyone has the gift of Evangelism. David Hubbard, a president of Fuller Seminary, helps define the difference:

> I admire people who can lead others to Jesus Christ right on the spot, who have the ability to turn every conversation into an occasion for sharing God's plan of salvation. I am not one of those, but I have a story to tell. (Peter Wagner, *Your Spiritual Gifts Can Help Your Church Grow,* p. 185)

Reflection

What do you feel are the most frequent situations in which people confuse roles and gifts?

Let's look now at several gifts of the Spirit. We will examine the rest in the next two lessons.

Hospitality

The gift of hospitality is mentioned in 1 Peter 4:9: "Use hospitality one to another without grudging." We know this is a spiritual gift because immediately after that verse Peter says, "As every man has received the gift, so minister the same to one another as good stewards of the manifold grace of God."

One definition of this gift:

> Joyfully and cordially meeting people's physical and emotional needs, particularly through food, lodging, and friendliness.

> I stood in the foyer of a small rural church five hours from home greeting members and visitors after my sermon. When the last person in line had waved goodbye, I looked around the sanctuary to find that my wife and I were the only ones left. I had not been at that church before, so I wondered how to lock up. More importantly, I wondered what we were going to eat for lunch. No one had asked us home to eat, and no potluck was scheduled. We were famished. We hadn't eaten since early morning, and it was a long, hungry drive home. That experience stands out in my mind (and stomach!) as if it were yesterday. The sting of abandonment and neglect. The utter lack of hospitality. That church may have had members who knew their Bibles inside out. They may have been extremely faithful in church attendance and tithe paying. But I didn't care one bit. All I knew was that they didn't give me any Special K loaf or mashed potatoes. How desperately that church needed people with the gift of Hospitality.

Thankfully, such an experience has been rare. I can't think of any gift that can do more to develop a sense of closeness among members and promote church growth than the wonderful gift of hospitality. When such people get busy, they can almost single-handedly change the whole atmosphere of a church.

Reflection

Tell about a time when other people's hospitality positively impacted your life.

Gift of Helps

The Apostle Paul mentions this vital gift in 1 Corinthians 12:28: "And God hath set some in the church . . .

[among them] the gift of helps."

One definition of this gift:

The ability to meet the practical, everyday needs of others around you through selfless service and assistance.

In the home of Lazarus, Martha practiced the gift of helps, sometimes to excess (Luke 10:40). In the early church, seven men with the gift of helps were chosen to guarantee an equitable distribution of food to the widows (Acts 6:3). The gift of helps is one of the most needed and, thankfully, most widespread gifts in the church. These are the folks who set up tables for potluck, clean the church, fix the boiler, take up the offering, arrange the flowers, cut out felts, and show up for work bees.

Intercession

This precious gift is mentioned in 1 Timothy 2:1: "I exhort therefore that first of all supplications, prayers and intercessions . . . be made for all men." James 5:13-15 also instructs us to intercede on behalf of the afflicted.

One definition of this gift:

The ability to gladly spend extended periods of time in prayer on behalf of others while exhibiting deep confidence in the workings of God.

There are individuals in the local church who sense a special call to pray for others. This quiet, behind-the-scenes gift, is one of the foundation stones for the work of the church.

If it were not for the gift of Intercessory Prayer, I would most likely not be a Seventh-day Adventist today. Raised a Methodist, I mowed the Adventist church lawn for years as a boy, but had no idea what went on inside that plain, aging building just down the street from home. During my junior year in high school, I studied Scripture with our Adventist neighbor, Elliot Towers, and was captivated by the Sabbath, the prophecies of Revelation, and the Second Coming of Christ. At the end of that year my folks, who saw Adventism as a dangerous cult, ordered me to return all my books and "not talk religion to Elliot ever again." Though terribly disappointed, I soon put Adventism into deep storage mentally.

Later I went to college in Boston to pursue a degree in engineering. After two years of undergrad math and computers, I felt a growing, inexplicable urge to dredge out my old Bible and review what I had learned with Mr. Towers three years before. Alone in my disheveled city apartment, I fumbled back over numerous texts, reflecting long on God's plan. Conviction haunted me.

After several months I summoned the courage to write to Elliot back on Cape Cod. "Dear Mr. Towers, I know we have not talked about religion for years, but I have been studying on my own, and I am very convicted that I should be a Seventh-day Adventist. More than that, I sense God wants me to be a pastor as well. Please let me know if this makes any sense." I swallowed hard and mailed the letter. One week later I received his reply. "Dear Kim, I was so thrilled to hear from you! I am not surprised at your decision. After your parents cut off our studies, I asked all the members in our little church to pray for you. When I drove to California I asked "prayer warriors" all the way out and back to pray for you as well. The Holy Spirit is now answering all those prayers in your behalf!" Within one year I became a theology major at Atlantic Union College and was baptized in the South Lancaster Village Church.

Reflection

Share a time when the gift of Intercession made a significant difference in your life or the life of someone you know.

Encouragement

In Romans 12:8 we read, "So we are to use our different gifts . . . if it is to encourage others, we should do so" (Good News Bible).

One definition of this gift:

The special ability to encourage, console, and reassure members of the body of Christ.

The King James Bible translates this gift as "exhortation." "Exhortation" does not capture well the true tone and tenor of the gift. The root meaning is best conveyed by our English word "encouragement." It is a gift that we see manifest markedly in the life of Barnabas. He was instrumental in launching Paul's ministry. Barnabas encouraged Paul, a recent convert, and the leaders in Jerusalem to meet and put aside their mutual distrust. It was also Barnabas who encouraged Mark to stay in ministry after Paul scolded him for running home to Mommy when the going got tough. If Barnabas had not used his gift of Encouragement, we might not have half the New Testament—Mark, of course, wrote our earliest Gospel, and Paul wrote thirteen epistles (Leslie Flynn, *19 Gifts of the Spirit,* p. 85-88).

Encouragement can be a very powerful gift for building up the church. My wife has been conducting an encouragement ministry for several years. Week after week she sends out carefully chosen cards filled with her thoughtful, uplifting messages to a variety of people—the young lady who gave special music, the people who go the second mile each week for potluck, the man who has not been to church in three weeks. My wife recently recruited two others to form an encouragement ministry team.

Reflection

Share an experience when someone's encouragement was particularly important to you personally.

Discernment

In Scripture this gift is referred to as the "discerning of spirits" (1 Corinthians 12:10).

One definition of this gift:

The special ability to distinguish spiritually between good and evil, genuine and false.

Christians with this gift seem to have a God-given sixth sense about things. They might be heard to say, "Something just doesn't smell right about this," or "I sense that this particular thing is good." Peter used this gift in his ministry when he affirmed the divinity of Christ. Jesus said, "Flesh and blood hath not revealed it unto thee, but My Father which is in heaven" (Matthew 16:17). Later on, Peter's gift of Discernment enabled him to unveil the deception of Ananias and Sapphira when they lied about their land (Acts 5:1-10). Such gifted Christians are also able to discern the genuine and false in the realm of ideas.

Faith

In 1 Corinthians 12:9 we read, "To another [is given the gift of] faith by the same Spirit."

One definition of this gift:

The ability to envision God's purposes and exhibit unusual confidence in His power to carry them out.

Paul exercised the gift of faith when he told the passengers on a storm-tossed boat, "So take heart, men, for I have faith in God that it will be exactly as I have been told [by Him]" (Acts 27:25 RSV). A classic example is George Muller, who operated five orphanages in England solely on faith. He built and maintained those orphanages, each housing 2,000 children, over a period of sixty years. Muller made his needs known only to God in prayer and through the gift of Faith received, during those many years, over 5 million dollars in donations (Leslie Flynn, *19 Gifts of the Spirit*, p. 141). The possessor of this gift will exercise faith not in their own plans, but in God's. They are often visionaries who can offer great encouragement by saying, "I know there are obstacles, but if we see God in it, let's go for it!"

Mercy

In his list of gifts in Romans, Paul instructs those with the gift of Mercy to use it with cheerfulness (Romans 12:8).

I like Peter Wagner's definition of this gift:

> The special God-given ability to feel genuine empathy and compassion for individuals, both Christian and non-Christian, who suffer distressing physical, mental or emotional problems, and to translate that compassion into cheerfully-done deeds that reflect Christ's love. (Peter Wagner, *Your Spiritual Gifts Can Help Your Church Grow,* p. 223)

One of my relatives teaches basic life skills to teens with severe emotional problems. A friend joyfully cares for people in the advanced stages of Alzheimer's disease. A visiting nurse compassionately tended to the many needs during the final days of my mother's life. Here is the gift of mercy at work as the voice and hands of Christ.

Review Questions

1. If you were starting a new church, what two ministries would you pray to be activated first?

2. In what ways could the nominating committee process be improved in order to move closer to running your church on the basis of spiritual gifts?

3. If people are divided up into visionaries, planners, and doers, which one best describes you?

Important Notice

Have a group potluck next week on the same night you study "Opening Your Gifts." Come one hour early. You may only bring foods that begin with the letter "S."

Love in Action

My Choice:

Make a list of five things from the Bible and/or Spirit of Prophecy about how important you are to God. Paste that list in a place where you can see it every day for a week.

Your Choice:

Did you eat too much at the group potluck tonight?!

Learning to be a Group: Your group will get much more out of its time together if each person covenants to specifically praying for the other group members during the week. At group meetings you can also help each other stay on the lesson topic during discussion as much as possible. And remember, confidentiality is a must.

Love in Action Feedback: Did that list of five ways you are important to God help get you through the week?

Ice Breaker: What is one of the riskiest things you have ever done? How did it turn out?

Opening Your Gifts

Christmas at Gramma and Grampa's! That tradition had remained unbroken for ten straight years, and the threat of snow could not deter the Mitchells from making it eleven. Henry and Susan hurriedly shuffled their excited brood of five children into the family's rusty station wagon early Christmas morning. Around legs and torsos they also crammed an intriguing variety of festive gifts for the kids and relatives.

Three hours later, after arriving safely and getting settled, Henry and Sue placed all the gifts under the glimmering tree. On signal, the children darted out from an adjoining room and searched for packages with their names. Paper and ribbon flew like birds startled from their nests. Shrieks of delight mingled with an occasional, "I can't believe I got it!" or "Man, wait till Johnny sees this!"

Amidst the din, four-year-old Karen kept circling the tree, sorting through the unopened packages, inspecting each label. After three circuits around the loot, she retreated to a distant corner, put her head in her hands and whimpered alone. Mom soon spotted the little one, sat down beside her, and asked what the trouble was. Karen sucked in a deep breath, looked up with teary eyes, and said, "Mommy, there aren't any gifts for me." Sue assured her that was not the case and began her own search of the significantly reduced pile. Sure enough, not one package was for Karen. Mom then realized that in the rush to leave home, one whole bag of gifts had been left behind. For Karen it was "the Christmas without gifts." Sue's heart broke when little Karen motioned for her to bend near and whispered, "I'm sorry if I wasn't good enough, Mommy."

Not good enough. Oh, how those life-sapping words have echoed in the hearts of thousands of church members who did not yet understand the nature of God's gracious love. God delights in giving gifts to His sin-ravaged children. He never leaves gifts at home. No one is ever overlooked. If we feel there are no gifts under heaven's tree for us, the problem is never with God. Either we don't have enough self-worth to believe He has put our name on that many presents, or we are not willing to accept them. Gift giving is based on God's goodness, not ours.

Reflection

Do you feel more comfortable receiving a gift or giving one? How do you think that might affect your ability to receive God's gifts for you?

In the God's kingdom, gifts are given for service. Because you are a minister, you have a ministry. God already has in mind a special place for you. Just like birds are made to fly and fish are made to swim, there is a ministry that is best suited to who you are. In order to live up to your potential, it is critical that you discover where you fit best within the body of Christ.

> I grew up in an old, old house. Every weekend my father and I worked at keeping the homestead from completely falling apart. Leaky faucets, a cellar wall that curved like a banana, doors that no longer closed, wires that mysteriously sparked—there was no shortage of projects. Dad considered it a personal defeat if he had to call in a professional to fix something. We tackled it all. We were enthusiastic but relatively unskilled. If something didn't fit, we just followed our trusty motto—"Jam it in!"

"Jam it in!" may work in a rickety house where mismatches only add to the home's character. But it does not work at all in churches. In order for our members to experience fulfillment in service for Christ, they must be matched well to ministry. Mismatches cause boredom and burnout. Mismatches make people feel used, draining their energy and enthusiasm for ministry.

How, then, can you find a ministry that is right for you? There are several key factors that can help you zero in on an effective area of ministry:

- Spiritual gifts
- Natural talents
- Passion
- Personality
- Experience

We'll look at each of these briefly.

Ministry Indicator #1—Spiritual Gifts

Your ministry should be in harmony with your spiritual gifts. The following steps will help you discover what spiritual gifts God has placed within you.

1. Study about spiritual gifts, especially those you think you might have. It's hard to find something if you don't know what you're looking for.

2. Take a spiritual gifts test and other assessments. A spiritual gifts test is a helpful guide, but only a guide. It is not an infallible indicator or the final word. It points the way and helps you focus. Because most spiritual gift tests are based on experience, they may not reveal gifts that are not yet used. Pinpointing gifts is a process that will probably take time.

3. Experiment with different ministries. Try different ways of ministering in order to discover where you are effective. This is a vital ingredient in gift discovery, yet many people are hesitant to experiment, usually because they are afraid to fail. That was the problem with the unprofitable servant in the parable of the talents in Matthew 25:14-30. This one-talent man didn't want to risk, so he didn't gain. Rather than investing his talent and putting it to use, he went to his backyard, dug a little hole, and dropped his one talent in. There it remained until the master returned. "Where is the talent I lent you?" the master inquired. "Good news," the servant replied. "I didn't take any chances with it. I buried it in a very safe place. Just go twenty paces north from the old oak tree behind my house, and

it'll be right there, four feet straight down. Great, huh?" "No, not great at all," the master replied, and he berated the man for sitting on such a valuable possession.

The real problem was the unprofitable servant's mental picture of the master. He was afraid to experiment because he pictured the master as a hard man. He said, "I know what kind of farmer you are. You try to reap where you haven't even planted any seeds" (see Matthew 25:24). If that were true, the master would be a terrible boss indeed. But the servant had it all wrong. The master was actually a generous and trusting man.

There is a lesson here for us today. Our own fear of failure is often rooted in a distorted picture of the Master. We see God as demanding, distant, intolerant of mistakes. But Christ doesn't berate us when we try and fall on our faces. He is the first one to dust us off, give us a hug of assurance, and whisper in our ears, "Great try!" He also places a safety net underneath us that says, "All things work together for good to them that love God" (Romans 8:28). We can experiment in various ministries without the debilitating effects of fear. One of the key truths of the parable of the talents is that, as far as God is concerned, "It is better to have tried and failed than to have never tried at all." God enjoys seeing us stretch, even if we flop.

Reflection

Tell about a memorable failure in your own life and what you learned from it.

I am no stranger to failure or its sting. Some episodes stand out in my mind as if they had happened yesterday.

When I was testing my new pastoral wings, I reluctantly accepted an unusual invitation to speak at an exclusive non-Adventist prep school for boys. On the night of the big speech I arrived at 5:30 p.m. for a finger-food buffet for the teachers and little ol' nervous me. After eating, we made our way to the large, ornate chapel. More than one hundred fifty teenagers filled the pews, along with a dozen scholarly faculty. Robed in black, I entered grandly behind the white-headed dean. Prayer, songs, and announcements unfolded, and then I found myself up in this lofty English pulpit.

I try to sprinkle a little humor in my youth sermons to keep attention. After telling one real-life knee slapper, the only chuckle I heard was my own silly giggle echoing off the hallowed rafters. I kept preaching, but my brain shouted, "Dud! You just told a real dud." I arrived at a very serious section of my talk, in which I recounted my "wild oat" childhood. This had just the opposite effect, creating an unnerving ripple of laughter. I paused to let the chuckles fade, then launched into another serious comment. This time the kids broke into an uproar. I had obviously gotten flustered and blurted out some unintended bit of humor. With 80 percent of my beleaguered sermon left to go, the audience treated me like some well-intentioned goofball. Sweating rivers from every pore, I skipped huge chunks of material and quickly brought my talk in for a bumpy landing.

I had failed. Self-pity companioned me. It took weeks back in my own church pulpit for my confidence to begin hobbling back. Sure, that experience hurt, but I learned tons about myself and how to give better talks. That failure made me more effective, and I have experienced much greater joy as a result. Failure can be a friend.

But really, why put ourselves through such risks? Why endure possible failure and pain? Is it worth it? Almost always the answer is Yes. We become happier, more fulfilled, more useful people as we stretch and grow. Many times new discoveries come through failure. Never forget the "147/805 Rule." The Wright brothers failed 147 times before they flew, and Edison failed 805 times before he invented the electric light.

I believe the words of Theodore Roosevelt are right on target:

> It is not the critic who counts; not the man who points out how the strong man stumbles, or where the doer of deeds could have done them better. The credit belongs to the man who is actually in the arena, whose face is marred by dust and sweat and blood; who strives valiantly . . . who spends himself in a worthy cause; who at best knows in the end the triumphs of high achievement and who at the worst, if he fails, at least fails while daring greatly, so that his place shall never be with those cold and timid souls who know neither victory nor defeat. (*Leadership,* vol. 15, no. 3, p. 93)

Reflection

How do you feel about trying new things? How often do you normally step outside of your "comfort zone"? When was the last time you did so?

---

4. Seek confirmation of your spiritual gifts from the body. As you seek to discover your spiritual gifts by experimenting with different ministries, ask people you trust to provide feedback on how you are doing. If you are truly gifted you will become increasingly effective, in your own way. I love to sing but also know I cannot do it well. My wife helps me resist the periodic urge to solo. Such self-knowledge spares both myself and others needless awkwardness. I warble happily, and quietly, in my pew.

I used to be terribly afraid of speaking in front of little kids. I imagined everyone booing and throwing huge, rotten tomatoes. One summer I foolishly agreed to be a camp pastor. To ease my nervousness when I gave my devotionals, I decided to show slides. I figured visuals would hold their attention and I could duck behind the screen if I flopped. Unfortunately, I forgot one crucial point in my planning—all the talks were outdoors. Bright sun washed the slides out so badly I had to describe virtually every detail. "If we could see this slide it would be a beautiful purple flower with. . . ." Desperate, I confronted my greatest fear and chose to tell an Eric B. Hare children's story about "rain that came up from the ground." I rehearsed for hours. At the next devotional I launched into the story with reckless abandon. Halfway through I thought, "Hey, no tomatoes." Later several kids told me they really enjoyed it. Three camp counselors told me they couldn't wait until the next story. I hadn't known I had it in me! I didn't, of course; God put it there. With courage born of confirmation from the body, I have enjoyed telling stories ever since.

Reflection

Frank has been head deacon for three years. He procrastinates and is terribly disorganized. Other deacons complain that he has no schedule for them to follow. Church repairs are often left undone. Frank has been spoken to about these weaknesses several times, without improvement. He says he feels called to this office. What should the body of Christ do?

Ministry Indicator #2—Natural Talents

Besides spiritual gifts, another indicator of where you can minister is the variety of natural talents God gave you at birth. These talents are not to be put aside when you become a Christian. God wants to use all of you for the advancement of His kingdom. People have all kinds of abilities that are valuable to the church—filing, landscaping, speaking, planning, repairing, cooking, painting, floral arranging, computer programming, sewing, interior design, conflict management, counseling, music, promotion, graphics, interviewing, organizing, and so on.

Ministry Indicator #3—Passion

One of the most critical indicators of where you will be most fulfilled in ministry is what Bruce Bugbee calls your "passion." He defines this as "the God-given desire of the heart to make a difference somewhere" (*What You Do Best In The Body of Christ*, Bruce Bugbee, p. 30). It has to do with what you care about most. Would you like to pour yourself into people needs—children, the elderly, the handicapped, the addicted, unwed mothers? Is there some cause that burns within your soul—hunger, illiteracy, the environment, drunk driving, racial prejudice, unemployment, missions? Is there some dream God has planted deep within your heart for where you want to serve?

Ministry Indicator #4—Personality

People come in a tremendous variety of personalities. The possibilities include people who are introverts or extroverts, organized or spontaneous, thinkers or feelers, up-front or behind-the-scenes, relationship-oriented or task-oriented. There are also the four basic temperaments: choleric, sanguine, phlegmatic, and melancholy—with combinations of each. Your ministry should match your personality and temperament in order for you to feel fulfilled. If the assistant cradle roll leader highly values organization, while the leader loves to "wing it," you may be headed for frustration. If the chairman of the finance committee is high on relationships but low on tasks, you may be in for a very long night.

> I am more of a thinker than a feeler, lean more toward things than people, and contain at least 90 percent melancholy. For quite a while I was emotionally drained by leading out each week in youth Sabbath school (about thirty teenagers). I started to get irritable about Friday noon. Friday night I'd reach for the antacid pills—"Why did I ever accept this job? I can't think of a single thing to do that really works." By Sabbath morning I could be a real Scrooge. I felt so ineffective. The nominating committee kept telling me that they couldn't possibly find anyone else. I gave it my best shot, and we did have some good times, but I was dying inside! Finally a terrific replacement came along (my hero), and I immediately gave my notice. Teenagers are vitally important, but the mismatch with my personality made me a round peg in a square hole.

The church needs to carefully link members to ministries that are in harmony with who they are.

Ministry Indicator #5—Experience

Experiences from your past can be another indicator of where you would minister best. One church has its members consider five areas of experience:

- Education
- Career
- Spiritual journey
- Previous ministries
- Painful events

(*The Purpose-Driven Church*, Rick Warren, p. 375)

Why repeat what has not been effective? Concentrate on your strengths. Experience helps focus our attention and sort out our choices. It adds the wisdom of reality to the idealism of our dreams.

In summary, as you seek to find your place of ministry, God provides enormous help. He asks you to reflect on the overall mosaic of your spiritual gifts, natural talents, passion, personality, and experience. Your ministry is too important to be left to chance.

Now let's look at a few more spiritual gifts.

Knowledge
In 1 Corinthians 12:8 we read, "to another [is given] the word of knowledge."

One definition of this gift:
The ability to understand biblical truth with unusual clarity and insight.

These folks are energized by learning, reading, and ferreting out truth. They would probably enjoy spending Saturday night reading the latest book on a certain topic. They are able to go deeper than the average person and connect various pieces of information into a coherent whole. Glib, cliche answers will not do. They challenge and inspire others to look more carefully at God's Word.

Wisdom
Paul tells us in 1 Corinthians 12:8, "For to one is given by the Spirit the word of wisdom."

One definition of this gift:
The ability to resolve life's problems and sort out difficult situations through the application of biblical truth.

The spiritual gifts of Knowledge and Wisdom may sound similar, but they are actually quite different. "Knowledge has to do with the discovery of truth, while wisdom has to do with its application to life" (Peter Wagner, *Your Spiritual Gifts Can Help Your Church Grow*, p. 218). The gift of Wisdom is intensely practical. These gifted ones are able get at the core of a problem and see through surface matters easily and quickly. A church that understands how the body of Christ is designed to function will make sure it has some of these people involved in making decisions.

Leadership
In Romans 12:6, 8 Paul counsels, "We have different gifts . . . if it is leadership, let him govern diligently" (NIV).

Peter Wagner gives a helpful definition of the gift of Leadership:

> The special ability to set goals in accordance with God's purpose for the future and to communicate those goals to others in such a way that they voluntarily and harmoniously work together to accomplish those goals for the glory of God. (Peter Wagner, *Your Spiritual Gifts Can Help Your Church Grow,* p. 162)

The New Testament knows only servant leadership: "And whosoever will be chief among you, let him be your servant" (Matthew 20:27). "Christian leadership is never dogmatic, demagogic, nor dictatorial. Rather, spiritual authority expresses itself in wisdom, tact, example, humility and service" (*19 Gifts of the Spirit*, Leslie Flynn, p. 126). Leadership is earned and bestowed, not grabbed or demanded.

I am convinced that effective leadership is vital for a group or organization to move forward. How often Old Testament Israel's spiritual well-being rose and fell according to the type of leadership they had. Gifted leadership brought the New Testament church successfully through enormous difficulties. Today, ministries in the local church often start up with great enthusiasm but later falter and fail because no one made sure the team included someone with the gift of Leadership.

Often pastors complain that they have very few leaders in their churches. I ask, "Would you know a leader if you saw one?" Usually we think of a leader as someone up front who has a rather choleric personality. A much better, more practical definition of a leader is "anyone who has followers." If that is true, then suddenly there are leaders all throughout our churches already. The Christian grandmother who teaches quilting to four people in her home is a leader. I also ask pastors, "Do you think leaders are dropped out of the sky like storks bring babies? What system do you have in place to discover and develop new leaders?"

Reflection

Recall one of the most effective non-pastoral leaders you have known. What characteristics made that person a good leader?

Administration

We read in 1 Corinthians 12:28, "In the church God has appointed . . . those with gifts of administration" (NIV).

One author defines the gift like this:

> The ability to organize and manage, working with and through others to achieve goals. (Bill Liversidge, *Principles of Church Growth,* p. 19)

A leader enables a group to figure out where it needs to go. A gifted administrator works out the details of how to get there. A pastor may not have this gift. Paper work piles up, phone calls go unanswered, meetings are disorganized and disjointed. Plans are made but not delegated or followed up. A wise church will allow its pastor to work his strengths and delegate his weaknesses. Rather than berating the pastor for not having the gift of Administration, a mature church will connect him with those who do have the gift and are willing to work as a team.

Teaching

In Romans 12:6, 7 we read, "We have different gifts . . . if it is teaching, let him teach" (NIV).

One author defines the gift like this:

> The ability to explain clearly and apply effectively the truth of the Word of God. (Leslie B. Flynn, *19 Gifts of the Spirit,* p. 74)

Jesus was, of course, the master Teacher. Matthew tells about the outdoor classroom in which Christ gave His life-changing Sermon on the Mount—"He began to teach them, saying . . ." (Matthew 5:2). He knew how to reach people of all backgrounds and temperaments. He could teach all three groups of learners—auditory (hearing), visual (seeing), and kinesthetic (doing).

Healing

In 1 Corinthians 12:9 we read, "To another . . . the gifts of healing by the same Spirit."

One helpful definition is this:

The divine enablement to be God's channel to restore people to health. (Bruce Bugbee, *Network,* p. 76)

Ray C. Stedman gives the proper breadth to this gift when he writes, "The word in the original Greek is in the plural, 'healings.' I take that to mean healing at every level of human need: bodily, emotionally and spiritually" (*Body Life*, p. 44, 45). At times healing takes place instantly, as in the days of the Apostles. More often healing occurs as a process, over time. A recent book about Dr. Ben Carson, the famous pediatric brain surgeon, was appropriately titled, *Gifted Hands*. Clearly such wonders in the operating room are the result of God's special blessing. People's lives and marriages have also been healed and made whole through the gifted intervention of Christian counselors and psychologists. Other Christians are used by God to restore individuals spiritually through the Word and earnest prayer. All of these gifts enable people to move beyond life's illnesses, scars, and struggles to new health of body, mind, and soul.

Review Questions

1. From what you have learned so far about spiritual gifts, what gifts do you feel should be present in each of the following ministries:
   - Church board
   - Strategic planning committee
   - Youth Sabbath school
   - Hospitality ministry

2. What is an ideal ministry in which you would like to be involved? If that is not happening at present, what stands in the way?

3. What two spiritual gifts does your church especially need more of at this time? Who is praying regularly for God to send them?

Important Notice

After studying this lesson together, the group should take time to pick members' names out of a hat before you head home. Then, during this week, think about one of the spiritual gifts you feel that person has. (Phone the group leader if you are unsure.) Purchase a small gift for the person, for not more than two dollars, that in some way symbolizes that spiritual gift. Bring it to the upcoming meeting when you study "Gift Wrap." At that meeting, time will be provided at the beginning to go around the circle, one by one, to give the gifts and explanations.

Learning to be a Group: Effective groups pay attention to the "climate" during the meetings. Does the meeting feel warm and inviting or kind of cool and reserved? Is it accepting or judgmental? Trusting or cautious? People grow best in an atmosphere that is safe.

Group Activity: Give each group member a small gift that symbolizes one of that person's spiritual gifts.

Gift Wrap

The time has come to "wrap things up" as far as our brief study of spiritual gifts is concerned. When people wrap up birthday and Christmas gifts, it is with the expectation that they will soon be opened and put to good use. I sincerely hope that will be your experience with spiritual gifts. This exciting topic deserves your continued attention.

Every Adventist church very much needs to learn how to function as a spiritual body in which all the gifts of the Spirit are discovered and used well. Whether or not that happens will depend on members like you and the priority you give to this endeavor. You can treat spiritual gifts like a picture that you hang on the wall and admire periodically. Or you can treat them like a new car that you get into and use over and over to take you where you need to go. So get behind the wheel and hit the gas!

One thing that discourages many people in their journey with spiritual gifts is that they run into some energy-sapping wrong turns and detours. Eventually they put spiritual gifts aside. We begin this week's study by looking at some of the most common sidetracks.

Wrong turns can be extremely aggravating.

> My fiancee, Ann, and I were to be wed in four days. Wednesday morning I bounded up the dorm steps to pick her up after a long, solo drive from the seminary. We had no time to waste. Winter break lasted only ten days, and we had to squeeze in a wedding rehearsal, wedding ceremony, reception, and honeymoon. The two of us were to arrive in New York City that evening for required routine tests before the doctor's office closed at 7:00. The test results in hand, we could then get our marriage license the next day, Thursday. Timing was crucial. Because of the holidays, the license bureau told us it would close right at 3:00 p.m. Thursday for the rest of the week.
>
> Wednesday evening we drove onto a vaguely familiar freeway in Queens, ahead of schedule and only minutes from the doctor's office. As we approached a fork, I quickly scanned the options on the overhead signs and sped left. A few minutes later, after whizzing through a maze of unfamiliar turns, we somehow faced the very same signs again. Somewhat surprised, I insisted that we take the same left. "Let me handle this, Honey. They don't call me Homing Pigeon Johnson for nothing!" A while later the same result. Stubbornly I took the same left a third time but then immediately tried an entirely different exit just ahead. This new maneuver looped us over and under and around, shooting us onto parkways, thruways, bypasses, and detours until we were hopelessly lost. As I motored past a huge construction project somewhere in the bowels of the inner city, I read 7:25 on the digital sign atop a bank nearby. No test tonight. Tired and worried, we eventually made our way to Ann's parents' home for the evening.

> The next day we called the doctor's office right away, apologized, and arranged for a 1:00 p.m. test, the absolute earliest slot available. The 3:00 p.m. deadline loomed before us. Time slipped away in the waiting room as our anxiety mounted. Each tick of the clock shouted, "Too late, Bozo. Should have allowed more time!" Ann's parents were at home praying, biting nails, and sweating bullets. Were we destined to suffer the dreadful embarrassment of a sham wedding ceremony without a license? At 2:30 p.m. the nurse finally brought out the precious test results. Ann and I burst out the door to catch a taxi for the race across town. I explained my emergency and told the driver I would make it worth his while if he made it. After careening through congested streets, we screeched to a stop at City Hall. Flustered, I forgot the tip and burst breathless into the clerk's office—with a full five minutes to spare.

Someday I'll learn to stop trusting my own inner map and warped sense of direction. I have spent so many needless hours meandering when I should have been arriving. There are also several wrong turns available to us when we try to understand and implement spiritual gifts. Over the years many well-meaning Christians have experienced unnecessary frustration by heading left when they should have motored right. Let's identify some needless detours.

Detour #1—Gift Projection

"Gift projection" is what happens when one person tries to make others feel they ought to have the same gift that person has. A person projects her gift onto those around her.

> Thousands of church members and visitors packed the large camp meeting building to hear the afternoon testimony of one of our denomination's great soul winners. He related stirring accounts of how he had led many people to Christ in airplanes, buses, hotel lobbies, taxi cabs, malls, and subways. He certainly had the spiritual gift of Evangelism. But at the end of his talk he said something that bothered me greatly: "There is not one of you out there today who couldn't do exactly as I have done, if you were right with God and were truly committed to saving souls. It's easy."
>
> I cringed. I thought all was well between me and my Maker, and I truly cared about the lost, but I couldn't hold a candle to this man's success in soul winning. Traditional soul winning had been a very awkward, difficult task for me. I now felt miserable. I must not be spiritual enough. I must not have mastered how to give my testimony well enough. I went home, prayed harder, and accosted a whole new crop of people with my testimony. They were turned off just as badly as those I offended before. The only good that came from it was that I finally gave away my last copy of the depressing tract, "Are You Really Ready to Face The Grim Reaper?" which went out of print during the Middle Ages.

Finally a wise friend delivered me from this misery by introducing me to spiritual gifts. "You know why you can't duplicate his success?" he said. "You don't have the spiritual gift of Evangelism. You have other valuable gifts, but that's not one of them. That fellow at camp meeting was making the common mistake of 'projecting' his gift onto everyone else. He doesn't understand spiritual gifts at all."

How freeing—I could be me and not what someone else thought I ought to be. The Apostle Paul made it clear that we are specialists in our area of giftedness when he said, "If the whole body were just an eye, how could it hear? And if it were only an ear, how could it smell?" (1 Corinthians 12:17, Good News Bible). We are not all alike. Paul goes on to say, "But now has God set the members every one of them in the body, as it has pleased Him" (1 Corinthians 12:18). Being *me* pleases God. It may not please the camp meeting speaker, but it pleases God. I can witness in ways suited to my own gifts and personality.

Church growth specialist Peter Wagner has the gifts of Knowledge and Teaching, but not the gift of Evangelism.

He offers a helpful insight when he writes of his experience on airplanes:

> I believe that a Christian who knows his or her gift-mix ought to structure as much time as possible to use that gift or gifts. Whenever I get on an airplane . . . I take 8 to 12 pounds of reading material [to develop the gift of knowledge]. . . . I look for a seat where no one is in the same row and consider it a good flight if I am alone. If someone sits next to me I make it a habit to pray and ask the Lord to keep that person quiet unless he or she has a heart that He has prepared for the gospel message. (*Spiritual Gifts Can Help Your Church Grow,* Peter Wagner, p. 183)

If the Lord does open the way, Wagner then gives his full attention to sharing his faith. He goes on to say, "The Lord is not going to hold me responsible for what I did as an evangelist, but He is going to hold me responsible for what I did as a scholar-teacher" (p. 183).

Reflection

Has a parent, spouse, or friend ever made you feel bad for struggling to do something that comes very easily to them? Is that a form of gift projection?

Detour #2—Gift Exaltation

Unfortunately the church has too often been guilty of exalting certain spiritual gifts far above their appropriate place within the body of Christ. For example, we sometimes exalt those gifts that place people up front on Sabbath morning. It may be the gift of Teaching in a Sabbath school lesson or sermon. It could be the gift of Music. Many members have talked to me in an almost apologetic way, saying that they only have gifts that work behind the scenes. "Oh, I could never stand up there and do what you do. I just do my own, puny little thing in the background." Sad.

I could give many illustrations from my years of pastoring to demonstrate that "quiet" gifts are extremely important. I remember one Sabbath in a wintery February when I got up to preach. Someone set the thermostat sky-high and forgot to turn it down. From the altar I couldn't get a deacon's attention at the rear of the church, and, being young, I didn't feel comfortable interrupting the sermon to mention the problem. Everyone sweltered in our own little holy hot house. People's interest melted. So many members slumped over and nodded off that it looked like a saintly slumber party. (Thankfully, no one snored!) A seemingly small bit of ministry to the thermostat would have saved the day.

> I especially remember the first baptism ever held in a country church I pastored. We used a portable baptismal tank, which we set up temporarily in the back room. Deacons shored up the dry rotted flooring. Because this baptism was a big deal, the conference president attended, along with interested members from neighboring churches. As the Friday night service began, one of the baptismal candidates entered the water next to me. The crowd pressed near. A deep sense of expectation permeated the old room. Everyone sang softly, "Just as I Am." Then, as I raised my hand to pronounce the baptismal blessing, the lights went out. We were plunged into inky blackness. The singing stopped. Reverence vanished as an annoyed voice from the crowd cried out, "Hey, anyone know where those stupid fuses are?" I stood there with the baptismal candidate in rapidly cooling water for what seemed like an eternity while some hero fixed the problem. When the lights flickered back on, I made some remark about the devil and the "forces of darkness" and in my heart thanked the Lord for my anonymous rescuer.

As another example of gift exaltation, we frequently place most of our outreach emphasis on reaping ministries. But in planning for a good harvest, any farmer knows that the long, hard work of clearing away rocks, plowing, planting, watering, fertilizing, and weeding have to be done first. Reaping is certainly more glorious than fertilizing. Reaping yields more obvious results than weeding. But reaping can, in one sense, be the easiest part of the entire process. If planting, watering, and weeding go well, the harvest is practically guaranteed.

If there are to be any heroes, they are the people who humbly plant and sow by loving others in the quietness of their homes, backyards, workplaces, and communities. They help prepare people's hearts, sometimes over years, for the reception of the Spirit. They probably have gifts such as Helps, Hospitality, or Mercy. These gifts are not glamorous. You will not hear the crowd cheer when these gifts are doing their work. But a keen ear can hear the angels sing. In the human scheme of things it will always be the man who carries the ball across the goal line who gets the crowd's adulation. But that is not God's view, nor should it be the church's.

Reflection

What can your church do to make the quiet, behind-the-scenes gifts feel more valued?

We desperately need to understand that we are a team. We are all important. Two years ago I somehow tore an entire fingernail off a finger. Oh, the pain! That finger became almost useless for weeks. Even multimillion-dollar football quarterbacks have been sidelined by a broken pinky. No one in the body of Christ should feel inferior. No Christian or ministry is second-class.

> I was reminded of this truth recently while reading about the person many consider to be the world's greatest living theoretical physicist, Stephen Hawking. The 51-year-old Hawking has been called a modern Einstein. He is a sought-after lecturer. He holds a prestigious teaching position at Cambridge University in England, where he is immersed in ongoing research. He is best-selling author as well, with a second book on the way. This list of accomplishments is all the more remarkable when one realizes that he suffers from Lou Gehrig's disease, which has left him almost completely paralyzed and unable to speak. He can only move some facial muscles and one finger on his left hand, which he uses to pick out words on a computer touch-screen attached to his wheelchair. One finger! If you have only one spiritual gift and feel like an insignificant finger in the body of Christ, remember Stephen Hawking. It is truly amazing what one finger has allowed him to achieve. (see A *Brief History of Time: A Reader's Companion,* Stephen Hawking, Bantom Books, 1992)

Detour #3—Gift Exclusiveness

"Gift exclusiveness" is a term for someone who says, "I'm only going to do things in the church that fit my spiritual gifts and nothing else. If I'm not gifted for it, I'm not doing it." It's true that guilt should not force us into a ministry. But neither can we ignore obvious needs and fail to pitch in during difficult times.

> Earlier this evening my daughter and I bought groceries. The checkout lines were rather long and slow. Near my feet I heard a rustling. I peered down and saw the store manager pick up some of those hand-held shopping baskets and stack them neatly by the entrance. Was that her job? Did she have to do that? No. But in order for things to run smoothly at that hectic moment, she pitched in and did something that was not part of her job description. For the good of the whole, she temporarily stepped out of her area of giftedness and served.

Likewise, regardless of our gifts, we need a servant spirit. The key is that when and how long we step outside our gifts should be our choice, a choice made without pressure. People who minister outside their gifts are at high risk for discouragement and burnout. Churches need to be sensitive to this danger and monitor these people's feelings carefully.

Reflection

How can we decide when to pitch in outside of our own gift-mix and when to say No?

Detour #4—Gift Immaturity

In Ephesians, Paul discusses spiritual gifts in chapter four, but his main emphasis is captured in the following verses:

> That Christ may dwell in your hearts by faith; that you, being rooted and grounded in love, may be able to comprehend with all saints what is the breadth, and length and depth, and height, and to know the love of Christ. . . . (Ephesians 3:17-19)

> . . . until we all attain to the unity of the faith and of the knowledge of the Son of God, to mature manhood, to the measure of the stature of the fulness of Christ. (Ephesians 4:13)

Some Christians mistakenly make spiritual gifts themselves the center of attention and forget the overall goal of growing up in Christ. Gifts are only a means to an end, not an end in themselves. Ellen White tells us what will happen when we put first things first:

> When those who profess to serve God follow Christ's example . . . when every act bears witness that they love God supremely and their neighbor as themselves, then will the church have power to move the world. (*Christ's Object Lessons,* p. 340)

Now, let's define more of God's spiritual gifts.

Craftsmanship

This special gift has been defined this way:

> The divine enablement to creatively design and/or construct items to be used for ministry. (Bruce Bugbee, *What You Do Best In The Body of Christ,* p. 61)

In Exodus 31:1-6 we read about the men God chose to oversee the building of the wilderness tabernacle. The Spirit of Prophecy tells us that "chosen men were especially endowed by God with skill and wisdom for the construction of the sacred building" (*Patriarchs and Prophets,* p. 345). God put Bezaleel in charge of the entire, fabulous project. The *Seventh-day Adventist Bible Commentary* adds, "He was to have not only the gift of creating designs but the ability to execute these designs" (vol. 1, p. 661). Many highly skilled laborers combined their efforts to build a place for God to dwell among His people. Some gifted artisans worked in metal and wood, while others made tapestries that were wondrous to behold. Members of the body of Christ today are also gifted artistically to bring glory to Him. From architecture to banners to floral designs, the worship and knowledge of God are creatively enhanced by these valuable craftsman among us.

Giving

In Romans 12:6-8 we read, "We have gifts that differ . . . he that gives must give with generosity" (Williams).

One definition of this gift:

The special ability to cheerfully give material resources, with unusual personal sacrifice, in Christ's stead, to those in need.

All Christians are supposed to give tithes and offerings to God. This is their spiritual role. There are, however, individuals whom God clearly calls to enter a deeper covenant of giving that requires special grace from the Spirit. Some unusual Christian businessmen have turned upwards of 90 percent of their company profits over to the Lord. Heaven can also inspire such singular sacrifice by lower income people. In 2 Corinthians 8:1, 2 the Apostle Paul speaks with gratitude of the churches in Macedonia: "How that in a great trial of affliction the abundance of their joy and their deep poverty abounded unto riches of their liberality."

I am reminded of one of my graduate school professors who developed his gift of Giving in a rather startling way. Nearing retirement, he and his wife lived in a tiny efficiency apartment in order to send as much of his salary to the those in need as possible. That is the same spirit Jesus commended in the widow when her little mite mingled with the shekels of the rich (Mark 12:41-44).

Music

One definition of this gift:

The special ability to glorify God and make Him known through the use of vocal or instrumental music.

Our minds immediately think of the many Psalms that David wrote, which were originally designed to be sung as a means of worship and praise. He also mastered the harp and played frequently for the king.

> [David's] mind was constantly penetrating into new depths, for fresh themes to inspire his song, and to wake the music of his harp. The rich melody of his voice poured out upon the air, echoed from the hills as if responsive to the rejoicing of the angel's songs in heaven. . . . His talents, as precious gifts from God, were employed to extol the glory of the divine Giver." (*Patriarchs and Prophets,* p. 669)

Jesus Himself had a beautiful voice.

> Often the dwellers in Nazareth heard His voice raised in praise and thanksgiving to God . . . and as His companions complained of weariness from labor, they were cheered by the sweet melody from His lips." (*The Desire of Ages,* p. 73)

Who can estimate the powerful, positive influence that music has played in the work of God on earth? From an old upright piano in a country church to the grandest choir, music has lifted hearts and encouraged countless souls.

Evangelism

This gift has been defined like this:

> The ability to share the Gospel with unbelievers in such a way that men and women respond and become followers of Jesus Christ. (Paul Ford, *Discovering Spiritual Gifts,* p. 21D)

Early in my pastoral labors I committed myself to team ministry. We raised funds locally to hire a full-time, experienced Bible worker to give studies and, most importantly, to train others. After much prayer, God gave us John, a wonderful, outgoing Christian, who came on board with the twin gifts of Teaching and Evangelism. He became a vital link in our attempts to reach young couples in the community for Christ.

I also remember one evangelistic team that stayed at our church for several months and held meetings that led more than 30 people to baptism. In our home visits, I rejoiced to see the gift of Evangelism at work through these team members as they carefully answered Bible questions and lovingly guided people of all ages to give their hearts to God.

I long for the time when churches learn how to activate the estimated 10 percent of their local members who have the gift of Evangelism. I long to see that gift used regularly throughout the year in coordination with the other gifts within the body.

Reflection

Recall a time when you were positively impacted by someone with the gift of evangelism. How did that gift affect you?

Pastor

In Ephesians 4:11 we read, "And His gifts were that some should be . . . pastors."

One definition of this gift:

> The special ability to guide, feed, and equip the members of the church in such a way that they develop a mature relationship with God and utilize their spiritual gifts in ministries of love.

The spiritual gift of Pastor is associated in Ephesians 4 with the related gift of Teaching. The Greek word for "pastor" is the same as that for "shepherd." Psalm 23 comes to mind, with its images of guarding and feeding the flock. In Ephesians, Paul indicates that the gift of Pastoring is similar to coaching. Someone with this gift builds other members up in three areas: knowledge of God, maturity of character, and ministry skill.

It is not always the case that someone occupying the "office" of pastor has the gift of Pastoring. A church in that situation can still be healthy if it learns to appreciate the pastor's other gifts and to look to lay-pastors for the spiritual gift of Pastoring.

Prophecy

Adventists are particularly aware of this spiritual gift because of its manifestation in the life and ministry of Ellen G. White. How valuable her work has been to the church in these last days. Through the centuries God has graciously guided His followers by giving timely messages through His prophets.

This gift has been defined like this:

> The special ability to "receive divine revelations from God to be communicated to men." (*Principles of Church Growth*, Bill Liversidge, p. 20)

This gift can be manifest in revealing the future or in giving a message that addresses a current need.

In these last three lessons I do not pretend to have covered all the possible spiritual gifts in Scripture. Different sources have different lists. It is now up to you and your church to arrive at a list that is generally agreed upon and then find ways to use those precious gifts of God's love.

Review Questions

1. As you are learning about the doctrine of spiritual gifts, you're reaction up to this point might best be characterized as: (choose one and tell why)
   a. Whoopee!
   b. Oh no!
   c. What's all the fuss?
   d. I'm thirsty for more.
   e. Go slow.

2. At this point, what spiritual gifts do you personally feel you might have?

3. What spiritual gifts in others have had the most impact on your own life? How?

For more information on spiritual gifts you may want to consult some of the books from which I have quoted in these last three lessons.

Love in Action

My Choice:

Have the entire group think up some project they can do together during the next week or two to benefit someone in need. The project should last no more than a couple of hours. Sunday mornings are usually good. You might rake an elderly person's leaves, paint a fence, clean out gutters, wash windows, etc.

Your Choice:

Learning to be a Group: Be slow to give advice and counsel on how others should deal with their problems. Be sure you have listened well and remember that you cannot fully appreciate someone else's struggles until you've walked a while in their shoes.

Love in Action Feedback: Did you find a group project to do together yet?

Group Activity: The Blind Circle.

The Orchestra

At some point in this lesson series people often begin to ask,

- How can the biblical concepts of church become a reality in our own congregation?
- How can our members become true priests and ministers?
- How can our pastor fulfill his role as equipper and coach?
- How can we fully activate the spiritual gifts in our midst?
- How can our church change?

Wonderful questions. In our search for credible answers, we should not fall into the trap of "one size fits all." Better to look more at principles than cookbook solutions. In this lesson we will examine a few issues that can help point the way.

Someone has commented that the seven last words of the church are, "We never did it that way before!" Change usually comes with difficulty for any of us, but especially for churches.

> Early in our meeting, an irate church board member glowered at me across the large table and jabbed his finger in my direction, spitting out his comments contemptuously. "As our pastor, how dare you desecrate the sanctuary of this church! You have absolutely no right to make the changes that you did. I certainly expected better of you." Desecrate? His words hit me like a blast of arctic air. My body tensed, and I instinctively leaned back a little. "I'm not sure what you mean," I replied, with as much outward calm as my churning insides would allow. "It's those pews," he continued. "You had no right to move the pews. They belong just where they've been for the past twenty years." Two nights earlier a couple of elders and I had removed two of the back pews on one side of the sanctuary to make room for a new Sabbath school class. I never imagined such a small deed would create such a huge problem. New to pastoring, I was long on renewal but short on church wisdom. Such was my introduction to the dynamics of change.

One of my favorite sayings is, "If you always do what you've always done, you'll always get what you always got." One definition of insanity is, "Doing the same thing over and over and expecting different results." Change is inevitable. We needn't change what works, but we dare not resist necessary changes. Church is a process, not a museum. Church is a living thing, not an artifact. Being church is like riding a bicycle: either you are moving forward or you fall.

Jesus Himself got into a bit of a tiff with the Pharisees over the subject of change. Among the many things they didn't like about His ministry was the fact that He and His disciples were experiencing too much joy (Matthew 9:14, 15). Isn't that one for the record books? They complained that Christ refused to get caught up in the dry formalism that suffocated Judaism. Jesus responded by sharing a marvelous insight into change:

> Neither is new wine put into old wineskins. If it is, the skins burst, and the wine is spilled, and the skins are destroyed. But new wine is put into fresh wineskins, and so both are preserved. (Matthew 9:17)

In those days there were no bottles, so liquids were kept in the skins of sheep or goats. (I wonder if they got five cents for turning in used skins at the market?) They sewed up the legs and used the neck of the skin as the opening to pour from. The new wine eventually gave off gases as it began to ferment. If they kept that new wine in old, dried up, inflexible wineskins, the gases would burst the skins apart. Both the container and contents would be lost. "Don't forget," Jesus said, "new wine has got to be put in new, flexible wineskins."

In this practical advice Jesus shares something profound about how to renew church. He is really describing *two* kinds of renewal. First there is the wine, which symbolizes new thinking and ideas. It represents personal renewal within our minds and hearts. I call this "personal" because it deals primarily with church members as individuals. The second type of renewal, the wineskins, is not nearly as familiar but equally as important. This type is organizational renewal. It has to do with how we organize ourselves as a local church to live out the new wine principles of the Word.

The new wine of Jesus' teachings could not fit into the old Jewish system. Soon the temple, the animal sacrifices and the Levitical priesthood, would all pass away and be replaced by the new, flexible wineskins and organization of the New Testament church. Keeping the old Jewish system would have been like putting a brand new Toyota or Chrysler engine in a 1920 Ford.

Jesus' point is that unless we renew both our ideas and the way we live them out as a church, the renewal will be short-lived. It is a fallacy to think you can effectively renew a church by simply renewing the individuals within it. You must also remodel the way those individuals function collectively as an organization. New truths cannot flourish in a "business as usual" atmosphere.

> I found an extreme example of the need for such two-fold renewal when I visited a local church Sabbath school some time ago. I felt as if I had entered a time warp. The "preliminaries" must have come directly out of the 1930s. I sat down in a straight-backed pew and listened incredulously as the secretary reported from up front the exact attendance last week in every division, children and adults. She carefully told us about last week's offerings—Birthday Thank, Sabbath School Expense, Missions—then analyzed the trends. We heard the stats on how many people studied their lesson last week compared to other weeks. She also re-capped the "preliminaries" from the previous week for anyone who might have missed. I chatted later with a gray-haired member next to me and found out that these reports were conscientiously given every week. I tried to imagine the "saint faint" that might occur if anyone tried to tamper with this venerable practice. They were faithful in preserving old forms but not so faithful in reaching people for Christ. Stagnant growth, empty pews. Where were the baby boomers? The teenagers? Where was anyone new?
>
> Suppose they drank some of that new wine Jesus talked about and understood that churches are supposed to be in the love and acceptance business, that our main purpose is to grow people. They would then need to find new wineskins to hold that truth. They would have to redesign Sabbath school to meet real people needs and foster in-depth, caring relationships. They could scrap the preliminaries altogether and go directly into classes that dealt with topics that scratch where people itch. They

could hold classes in circles rather than pews so that people could hear each other and develop a sense of closeness. If people really believe God is creative and alive, they will not present Him in a dead and boring form. New wine requires new wineskins.

Reflection

What significant positive changes have occurred in the way your church functions during the past five years? What does this tell you about how your church relates to change?

Moses found organizational renewal vital to success when God called him to pastor the weak, very imperfect, church of Israel. He preached earnestly about God's "new wine" and labored intensely. But as the people came to him day after day with their complaints, he grew uptight and frustrated. He felt overwhelmed and found himself on the fast track to burnout. Working harder didn't make church better. The solution? Surprisingly, God spoke through Jethro to bring Moses' strategy into balance. In effect Jethro says, "Moses, you've got to pay attention to the wineskins. Examine how you've organized things. I want you to develop leaders over thousands, leaders over hundreds, fifties, and tens" (Exodus 18:21). Moses might have replied, "Hey, that's just a lot of management mumbo jumbo. I'll just pray more fervently and put in longer hours. I don't need a lecture on organization!" Instead he took Jethro's advice seriously, and the problem was solved.

Many pastors and local leaders today face the same problem Moses did centuries ago. Their church is not well, and despite their best efforts, not much seems to improve. The symptoms may include anemic growth, a few tired members doing all the work, losing members out the back door, financial struggles, a handful attending prayer meeting, routine worship services, the same tired litany of programs. In an attempt to remedy the situation, we often adopt the approach Moses was using before Jethro expanded his thinking. Pastors preach harder, and the faithful core work and pray harder, with the same limited results. Once again, the answer often lies in paying attention to the wineskins, in renewing how the church functions as an organization.

We have to pay attention to organizational issues because "church" is far more than a collection of spiritual individuals. "Church" involves being and doing far more together than we ever could alone.

> The other day our local news carried the story of the 100th running of the Boston Marathon. Over 40,000 runners entered the exhausting twenty-six mile race from the outskirts of the city to downtown. There were so many participants that by the time the first runners were miles down the course, the last runners in line were just starting. When the gun fired, this massive wave of humanity surged forward, each person with his or her eye on the goal. They all exerted extraordinary effort, with one purpose in mind.
>
> Many people think the local church is similar to a marathon—a collection of 50, 100, or 500 people all racing toward the heavenly prize. The problem with this analogy is that even though the marathon runners are on the same road at the same time, they are still simply a collection of individuals. None of the runners is really depending on the others. They benefit from the morale boost, but the runners are not truly interconnected. Church shouldn't be like that at all.

Church is supposed to be more like a team of climbers trying to conquer Mt. Everest. As in the marathon, they all have the same goal, but now they must coordinate their efforts. It would be literally impossible for any one of them to climb that mountain alone. Each of the climbers is in excellent condition individually. But success depends on their ability to function together.

The Parable of the Orchestra

God calls His church today to an extremely high mission, which can only be accomplished together. He asks us to collectively reveal His glory, which is His love, to the world. God wants each local church to operate like a spiritual orchestra to present the stirring melody of His glory to the community. The members are the musicians, and the pastor is the conductor.

> Unto Him be glory in the church by Christ Jesus. . . . (Ephesians 3:21)

> From the beginning it has been God's plan that through His church shall be reflected to the world His fullness and His sufficiency. The members of the church, those whom He has called out of darkness into His marvelous light, are to show forth His glory. The church is the repository of the riches of the grace of Christ; and through the church will eventually be made manifest . . . the final and full display of the love of God. (*Acts of the Apostles,* p. 9)

Sadly, however, churches often fall short of His lofty purpose, leaving the music badly distorted. The parable of the orchestra illustrates the problem.

"Look Carl, a new orchestra is coming to town and putting on a benefit concert next week. They're playing a composition entitled 'The Glory of God.' I hear it's an incredible piece of music written by a famous composer who lived about 2,000 years ago. Can we go?" Mary shows the eye-catching ad to her husband, The big advertisement announces:

> **The Good News Orchestra**
> **presents**
> # The Glory of God
> Come hear the most marvelous music ever composed in all its soul stirring power and splendor!

Carl and his wife mark their calendars. So do hundreds of others. Reservations are brisk. The ad worked well.

On opening night the concert hall is buzzing with activity. A local radio station has decided to broadcast live. People from all walks of life, from near and far, have been captivated by the promise of a gala evening of wonderful music.

One young concertgoer notes, "Hey, Mom, in the program it says the music opens with a 'grand allegro movement.' That means everyone plays together really loud and fast, doesn't it?" The mother simply holds one finger up to her lips and nods.

Seats fill, lights dim, and the curtain rises. After scanning the hundred-member orchestra, one lady in the audience whispers to her spouse, "Dear, why are there so many empty chairs?" Her husband offers, "They were obviously expecting some musicians who didn't show." "Oh, how disappointing," she sighs.

Another obvious problem is that several of the cello players are sitting in the trumpet section. Half the flutes are standing in back with the percussion players. In fact, only a handful of musicians are in their proper places.

Soon the conductor strides to center stage smiling, steps onto the podium, and bows graciously to expectant applause. After a dramatic pause, he taps his baton on the music stand, holds his arms out, then beats the air animatedly to begin the evening's concert. Only about a third of the players respond. They earnestly try to make great music, but most of them, unfortunately, are not on the same page. Others have the wrong music entirely. Several are using their instruments in odd ways. Four violin players are holding their violins upside down on their laps, tapping on the back like a drum. Two clarinet players are blowing in the wrong end of their instruments. The other two-thirds of the orchestra appear completely distracted. Several are sipping sodas. Another is clipping his nails. Others are reading, playing games, or chatting.

Amidst the din, the conductor tries desperately to get things on track. Letting out a loud sigh, he grabs a tuba and takes up a position behind the cellos. He blasts out a series of low, growly notes that echo through the hall. Red-faced and out of breath, he stops, looks around at the musicians, then leans back in his chair in frustration. The orchestra's meandering music swirls about him. In an attempt to salvage the concert, the conductor runs through the orchestra, frantically playing various unused instruments himself.

At one point, a percussionist takes it upon himself to step to the front of the stage and beat his own drum insistently. He is coaxed back to his place by friends. After a while several of the players who had been spectators choose to get involved. One group of ten forms a circle on the right side of the stage and plays their own country music favorites. Another group heads into the audience and starts selling popcorn and cold drinks.

Several musicians do seem to be competently playing the right music with the right instruments. They are unable, however, to produce much glory on their own. They are overshadowed by the lack of overall coordination. A half dozen musicians stand, pack their instruments, and march out in disgust.

In desperation, the orchestra leader runs back to the podium, waves the baton in exaggerated looping motions, then stops, shakes his head, and flings the baton aside.

The next day's newspaper reviews are merciless. One editor comments, "Rarely have I witnessed such a distressing gap between promise and reality." Another writes, "My disappointment is great. Such potential squandered. This certainly cannot be what the original composer had in mind."

How can this ineffective orchestra be fixed? Would it help if the musicians took more music lessons and improved their ability to play? Yes, that would help some, of course. The key here, however, is to see that increasing the effectiveness of the individual musicians would still leave us a long way from success. The problems revolve around how the orchestra functions together. They would have to pay attention to the following wineskin issues:

- The musicians should discuss together what values and priorities are essential for them to be successful as an orchestra.
- Everyone needs to share a clear, common vision of what they want their orchestra to be.
- Rather than playing the musicians' instruments for them, the conductor needs to focus primarily on putting together an overall strategy and equipping leaders within the orchestra who can pull each section together.
- The musicians who understand best how to be an orchestra should mentor those who do not.
- Orchestra members should be interviewed, listened to, and assessed to see if they are playing the right instrument. They need to find where they can function best.
- The musicians need to be shown how to function together as a team and blend their part of the music into the whole.

- A process of ongoing feedback, encouragement, and accountability needs to be in place.

The same issues, when understood and applied, can breathe new life into the local church.

Reflection

What aspects of this parable and accompanying suggestions relate to your church? What changes do you sense God is calling your church to make in order to create great music?

The Apostle Paul understood the importance of organizational renewal, which he highlights throughout 1 Corinthians 12. Paul points out that church is supposed to be organized like our human body. It was a real eye-opener for me to understand that, like the human body, "church" has systems on the inside that need to be working well in order for there to be biblical health. When I look at my own body I see the obvious—skin, flab, legs, arms, a balding head. But when a physician looks at me he thinks about all the different parts or systems inside that enable me to function well. There is the digestive system that turns mashed potatoes and chocolate chip cookies into cell food. There is the nervous system that allows my big toe to send e-mail to my brain. I also have a circulatory system, respiratory system, reproductive system, skeletal system, and muscle system, to name just a few. Amazing. Is it any wonder that churches ache, wheeze, and stumble when several of these systems are malfunctioning, or worse, missing entirely?

Too often churches deal only with outward symptoms. They have to guess at solutions. Suppose I went to my doctor with some pain, and without doing any exams or lab tests, he said, "Hey, Kim, I've got these pretty little purple pills here that helped people in other parts of the country. Why don't you pop a few and let me know what happens." I'd think that guy was a quack. And yet how often we do that when trying to fix the church. "Hey, I heard a congregation over in Kansas used this program, and it did wonders." And if that doesn't work, we try another. Grab bag. The purple pill syndrome. We need to look beyond the surface and understand what's going on inside.

The situation is similar to that of fixing cars. I know almost nothing about automobiles. During my growing up years, dad was the mechanic, and I held the flashlight. "Point that thing over here, Bub [dad always called me Bub]. Good, that's it, hold the it right there." (It's because of that early training that I can aim a flashlight today with great accuracy.) Anyway, that was as close as I ever got to being an mechanic. I know the engine is up front, the gas tank is in the back where you put the gas station nozzle, the shift thing is on the floor, the clutch is on the left—you get the drift. I see only the obvious. If my car makes a weird noise or starts blowing smoke out the back, I don't have a clue. "Why" is a total mystery.

But when a mechanic looks at my car, that's different. The critical difference between him and me is that in his mind he pictures the insides. He knows my car is supposed to be organized into various systems. There is the exhaust system, electrical system, fuel system, cooling system, motor, drive train (not an actual train!), the transmission, and so on. He runs tests and checks things out. Because he understands how cars should be put together, he can diagnose properly and repair. If your church is blowing smoke, simply kicking the tires won't help. You have to pay attention to what's going on under the hood.

By way of illustration, let's take an in-depth look at just a couple of key church "systems" that are often missing or in need of extensive repair. The following examples—(1) assimilation and (2) ministry placement—typify the wineskin issues that churches should examine in order to experience deep, lasting health.

Assimilation

The Adventist church's bucket has some big holes in it. We keep pouring people in the top, and they keep leaking out the bottom. At least a third of those who join our church eventually stop coming. And too many who remain never really feel connected to those around them. They don't become "assimilated" into church life. So how easy is it for people in your church, especially new people, to develop a sense of belonging? How is that system functioning? To answer those vital questions, many have found it helpful to examine their church according to the two circles pictured below:

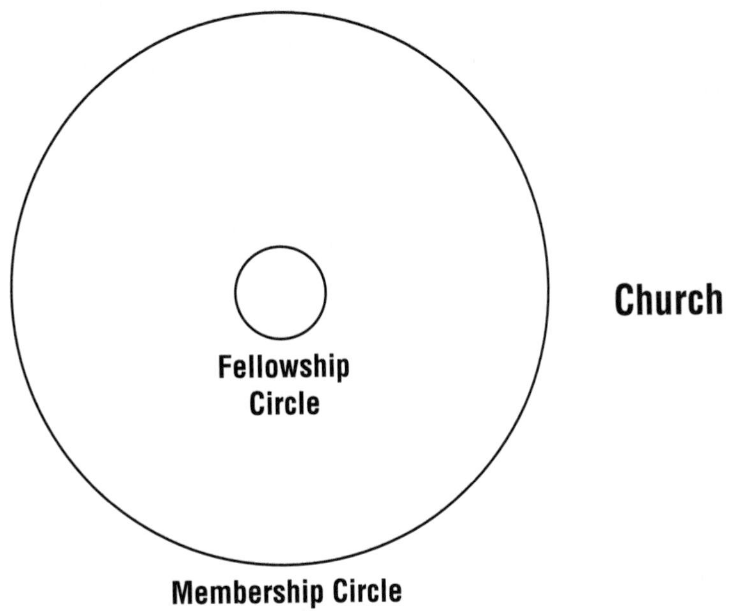

(Lyle Schaller, *Assimilating New Members*, p. 81)

The larger of the two circles is the Membership Circle. You get inside that circle by joining a local church through baptism or transfer. If your name is on the books, you are in the Membership Circle. Inside of that is the smaller Fellowship Circle. People inside here have developed friendships and support networks and feel as if they are accepted and meaningfully involved in church. They fit in. One pastor visited all his members and asked them to put an "X" where they thought they were on this chart. One man put his "X" way outside the Membership Circle. The pastor thought he misunderstood and told him, "Joe, you are a member here, you are already inside that outer circle." "No," he replied, "my name may be on the books, but I don't feel like I am a member at all. I feel like an outsider." Most of the other "X's" in the pastor's survey fell somewhere between the inner and outer circle, with the minority in the center (Lyle E. Schaller, *Assimilating New Members*, p. 73).

There are several points here for your church to ponder:

1. People inside the Fellowship Circle almost always underestimate the number of members who feel they are not. They also underestimate how difficult it is to get into the Fellowship Circle. People on the inside feel that the line that makes up the Fellowship Circle is as easy to cross as the lines painted on a gym floor. To someone on the outside, however, that line looks like a ten-foot fence. If you want to know how accepting your church really is, ask the visitors who never came back and the members

who dropped out.

2. The best way to get people into the Fellowship Circle is through friendships. Small groups can be especially helpful. Another excellent pathway is to involve people in a meaningful task or ministry. The first six months are critical.

3. No matter where they put their "X" today, every member is mentally and spiritually either moving closer to the center or closer to the outside. They may attend church regularly and sing in the choir but be headed outward in their hearts and minds. How do you think your church could discover as early as possible which way people are headed? How could you help them turn around?

4. The ideal is for the Fellowship Circle to be the same size as the Membership Circle. That is unrealistic but worth striving for. The two circles won't come much closer, however, unless you intentionally organize to make it happen. Fail to plan here, and you plan to fail. How big is the Fellowship Circle in your church? How can you be sure? How easy is it to enter?

Many sincere, dedicated members remain on the edges of church life simply because the church has failed to organize an effective assimilation process. People's emotional needs are as real as physical hunger. Until the church is able to meet those needs for acceptance and support, it will make little meaningful progress in its attempts at renewal.

Reflection

Where would you place your "X" on the Membership and Fellowship Circles? Why?

Ministry Placement

A new pastor presented his church leadership with a tremendous challenge. "What would happen," he said, "if we decided to take the biblical doctrine of the priesthood of all believers seriously?" At that time very little was known about how to help the laity become involved in meaningful ministry, but they accepted the challenge nonetheless. By trial and error they pressed through a multitude of discouragements and difficulties. Over the next ten years their church witnessed an explosion of lay ministries. The church grew from 200 to its current membership of 1,300. The key? They chose to remodel how they did church. They paid attention to the wine-skins as well as the wine. They reorganized so they could care for their most precious resource—people. They developed a ministry placement process to help people discover their spiritual gifts and find an effective ministry.

In that placement process, the church takes time to help members understand God's vision for church, much like you are doing in this small-group series. They interview every member, giving each person assessments for discovering gifts, talents, and areas of interest. Based on the interview and test results, members are given the opportunity to experiment with various ministries, under careful tutelage and mentoring, until they find their niche. They receive all the help and ongoing training they need to be successful, as well as loving feedback and encouragement throughout the entire year (adapted from *The Starter Kit*, Leadership Training Network, p. 1-21).

Too many enthusiastic Adventist Christians have become staunch spectators because the church didn't learn how to handle its people resources well. Putting people in the wrong ministry, cramming square pegs into round holes, can drain spiritual energy. Assigning people to a ministry with no training or support can discourage even the most dedicated individuals. Members who are labeled as uncommitted are often simply living out the old adage, "Once burned, twice shy." Having a poorly organized or nonexistent ministry placement process can unwittingly lead to the very Laodicean condition we so earnestly decry. To preach and pray for personal renewal among the members while neglecting organizational renewal is like putting one foot on the gas and the other on the brake.

Reflection

What aspects of the ministry placement process described above does your church need to work on the most? How can you get started?

Along with assimilation and ministry placement, some of the other systems your church could examine are these:

- Intercession—Has your church activated those with the spiritual gift of Intercession to undergird all you undertake with prayer?
- Visioning—Does your church have a clear, captivating, well-understood vision for the future?
- Strategic Planning—Do you have goals and plans to accomplish your vision? Do you know where the church wants to be in five years? Ten years?
- Leadership Development—Do you have some way to recognize, cultivate, and train new leaders at all levels? How are you equipping and maturing current leaders?
- Small Groups—Does your church provide small groups in which people can find help with their problems and support for personal growth?
- Outreach—Are you training members to form friendships with non-Adventists? Is there a steady stream of visitors to your church from the community? Is outreach an event or a process?
- Worship—Is the worship service creative and uplifting? Does it meet the varied needs within the congregation?

Like a good physician or mechanic you should now be able to analyze your church in a more complete way. If your church is ailing, look over the systems listed above and see which areas might be in need of attention. Don't feel overwhelmed or tackle change all at once. The process of organizational renewal involves prioritizing different areas, breaking them down into bite-size pieces, learning how they ought to function, and patiently making improvements as the Spirit opens the way. Leaders especially need to make these topics a central concern. Church life and health depend on it. How fast your church travels toward wholeness is not as important as the fact that you are headed in the right direction. The road to recovery is not easy, but can be extremely rewarding as the body of Christ begins to comes alive.

Review Questions

1. After reading this lesson, how would you assess the health of your church? What will it take for your church to get on the road to lasting, biblical renewal? How can you help?

2. If I joined your church, what could you guarantee would happen in the next six months to make sure that I felt properly assimilated? How would my needs for new friends, involvement, and support be cared for?

3. React to the following statement: ". . . the key issue for churches in the twenty-first century will be church health, not church growth. . . . Healthy churches don't need gimmicks to grow—they grow naturally." (Rick Warren, *The Purpose-Driven Church,* p. 17)

Love in Action

My Choice:

Choose a church member who seems to feel outside the Fellowship Circle of your church. Do something this week to help the person feel more included.

Your Choice:

Learning to be a Group: There are various roles that different people can play in a group—Encourager, Tension Reliever, Communication Helper, Harmonizer, Summarizer, Information Giver, Information Seeker, Hospitality Giver, Trust Builder, Process Observer, Reminder, Schedule Keeper, to name a few. (see *Joining Together*, David W. Johnson and Frank P. Johnson, p. 26, 27)

Love in Action Feedback: Were you able to help someone move closer to the Fellowship Circle of your church?

Ice Breaker: What has been one of your more humorous or embarrassing moments in life?

The Kiss

David nervously scanned the riverbank as his Special Forces patrol navigated the hostile waters of a Vietnamese river. He and his fellow soldiers were headed back to the previous day's battle scene in a six-man raft to obtain an accurate enemy body count, the only true measure of success. Suddenly, shots pierced the sultry air from the thick underbrush on the left bank. Dave instinctively grabbed a phosphorous grenade and pulled the pin. Just as he cocked his arm back beside his ear, a bullet hit the grenade, exploding it in a horrific flash of pale blue light and searing heat. The blast instantly incinerated half of David's face, demolished several fingers, and mangled his arm and shoulder area. He fell limply into the river, where the water caused the phosphorous to burn even more fiercely. Somehow he struggled to shore, crawled up the muddy embankment, and lapsed into unconsciousness.

When the firefight subsided, the other soldiers hurried to David's aid. After a brief examination of his sickening wounds, they pronounced him dead and called in the medical helicopter. As the medics carried Dave back to the chopper, his upper body, still encrusted with patches of hot, sticky phosphorous, burned right through the stretcher. He revived on the flight back to base but could not talk because of a hole in his windpipe. He slowly placed one palm over the opening and made a desperate gurgling sound for help. The startled medics, who had also marked him dead, nearly jumped out the helicopter door.

After extensive surgery and agonizing days in the base hospital, Dave was informed that his young bride would be flown in soon from the States. Tears of hope mingled with deep anxiety. In the large, open ward of disfigured soldiers, wife after wife had rushed to her spouse's bedside, only to recoil in disgust, throw their wedding ring on the bed, and hurry from the awful room in tears. David knew his wounds were the worst. His chest heaved in great sobs as he mourned his physical loss and the likelihood of losing his sweetheart and best friend as well.

As the fateful day approached, he rehearsed a speech he had created in the desperate hope that something he could say would convince his wife to accept him. The morning of her arrival, Dave watched the ward entrance intently. Then she stood framed in the doorway. As she made her way to his side, Dave forgot his speech and could only manage to blurt out, "I'm sorry for the way I look ." His wife paused, then bent over and kissed him on the part of his face that had been burned the worst. Her soft lips pressed against melted flesh and oozing sores. She smiled and said, "What makes you think I married you for your looks anyway?" And the healing began, the deep healing that only true acceptance can bring. She accepted him long before he felt acceptable.

So it is in the spiritual realm that a sense of acceptance with God forms the basis for the rest of our Christian lives.

Without it we can be secretly running scared—never secure and never free. Unless we discover how to find such acceptance and security in Christ, we cannot fully participate in His marvelous plan for us or His church.

In Isaiah the Lord describes us as spiritual lepers:

> The whole head is sick, and the whole heart faint. From the sole of the foot even unto the head there is no soundness in it: but wounds, and bruises and putrefying sores. (Isaiah 1:5-6)

Like Dave, we're not a pretty sight. No one's going to win any spiritual beauty contests here. But notice from Scripture how Christ relates to lepers.

> A pathetic, dirty, stinking leper nervously hobbles within earshot of Christ. His putrefying flesh repulses the other people who have gathered for healing. Desperately clinging to one last hope, the leper yells, "Lord, if You will, You can make me clean." The man reaches out one arm before him and stumbles closer, as sobs pour forth from years of loneliness and hurt. The crowd recoils, stepping on each other in retreat, shooing the children ahead. Jesus comes forward, His piercing gaze fixed on the leper's every move. Our Lord's loving eyes fill with tears as He stands next to the victim and gently places his hand on the man's rotting shoulder. Then He utters those wonderful words, "I will, be thou clean."
>
> Jesus could have healed the leper from a distance, but He understood the more important work of healing the inner man. In that touch, Christ overcame years of shame. He accepted the leper before the leper was acceptable, before the leper even accepted himself (see Mark 1:40).

The Trinity is not turned off by sinners. When Judas came to betray Jesus in the garden, Christ called him "friend." Jesus' enemies inadvertently paid Him the greatest possible compliment when they labeled Him a "friend of sinners." The Trinity does not say, "Shape up so we can accept you." Instead, they say, "We'll accept you so you can shape up." While we were still mucking around in a spiritual sewer, God personally invited us to His elegant banquet.

God wants us to be *sure* that we are members of His family. He is not glorified by our uncertainty. It is not humble to be unsure of our salvation. How do you think I would feel if someone asked my daughter if she belonged to our family, and she replied, "I hope so." Hope so? If she said that, I'd feel terrible. I want her to be able to say, "Yes!"

The Apostle John didn't want his readers to say "hope so." He wanted them to be sure of salvation.

> These things have I written unto you that believe on the name of the Son of God that ye may know that ye have eternal life, and that ye may believe on the . . . name of the Son of God. (1 John 5:13,14)

So how can we *know* we're really accepted? How can we be sure that we have eternal life? What we need to be saved is to accept God's loving invitation to enter into a trust relationship with Him based on fundamental truths. Those truths are revealed most fully in the life and death of Christ.

> Suppose your name is Bob. You tell me, "Kim, I'm not really sure I have the assurance of salvation. I would love to have the confidence that I am a member of God's family. How can it happen?" I invite you to come with me to Calvary. As we stand there staring at Jesus on the blood-stained cross, I highlight certain key truths:

Bob, do you know that Jesus loves you more than you can imagine? When Christ cried out from the cross, "My God, My God, why have You forsaken Me?" He was experiencing separation from God. He was experiencing what we deserve because of our sin. He took our place, dying the death that should have been ours. As Christ bore our sins on Calvary, He thought He would be separated from His heavenly Father for all eternity. Jesus loves you so much that He was willing to go into the grave forever that you might be in heaven forever.

And Bob, just as our sin separated Christ from His Father, it does the same to us. Sin causes us to run from God and live apart from Him.

Also Bob, isn't it amazing how terribly human beings treated Christ? How could they reject Him and torture Him to death? It was their sinful human hearts that put selfishness on the throne of their lives instead of God. Unfortunately we have the same sinful nature in us that was inside of them. We cannot save ourselves or change our hearts; only God can. He must be in charge.

Finally, God longs to heal our broken relationship with Him and make us part of His family. He wants to adopt you and me. Bob, do these lessons make sense to you? If they do, then let's offer this simple prayer and trust God for the answer:

Lord, take my heart; for I cannot give it. It is Thy property. Keep it pure, for I cannot keep it for Thee. Save me in spite of myself, my weak, unchristlike self. Mold me, fashion me, raise me into a pure and holy atmosphere, where the rich current of Thy love can flow through my soul. (*Christ's Object Lessons,* p. 159)

According to the promises of God, you are now part of God's family. You have God's gift of eternal life. Listen to these encouraging words:

> If we confess our sins, he is faithful and just to forgive us our sins, and to cleanse us from all unrighteousness. (1 John 1:9)

> You confess your sins and give yourself to God. You will [choose] to serve Him. Just as surely as you do this, God will fulfill His word to you. If you believe the promise—believe that you are forgiven and cleansed—God supplies the fact; you are made whole, just as Christ gave the paralytic power to walk when the man believed that he was healed. It is so if you believe it. (*Steps to Christ,* p. 53)

You have experienced the new birth! More important than mouthing the words is for the words to express the desires of your heart. As you learn about Christ, you begin to see things as God sees them. You experience repentance and faith. Repentance is turning away from selfishness; faith is turning toward God. Our faith doesn't earn us anything. We are actually saved by God's grace, which is accepted through faith. We say we are saved "by faith" in the sense that faith is the conduit, the connection, by which we receive heaven's most gracious Gift, Jesus Christ. You used to be closed to God, now you are open. You used to be in a far country, now you are home. You begin a trust relationship with Christ and are safe in Him.

Reflection

Name a time in your life when you felt truly valued and accepted by another person.

Over the years I have found, both in my own life and those of others, certain barriers to having full assurance of salvation. We'll touch on some of those barriers in this lesson.

Assurance Barrier #1: Legalism

One of the greatest hindrances to fully experiencing the assurance of salvation is legalism in both its obvious and subtle forms. The obvious definition of legalism is the belief that one can earn salvation by one's own behavior. Most Adventists would reject that kind of blatant legalism immediately. The problem is that we can mouth the right words about grace and faith and yet be infected with other, less obvious forms of legalism that are just as lethal to assurance.

A root of legalism is the misunderstanding of how the Bible defines sin. We sometimes define sin incorrectly as primarily something we *do*—sinful behaviors. Spiritual growth largely becomes a process of overcoming a mental list of sinful deeds. The infinite, enormously varied, and colorful pallet of love gets reduced to a gray list of prohibitions. Focusing on sin as mainly something we do creates an attitude that makes it difficult for a person to fully comprehend grace. It opens the way for the following four problems:

A. **Assurance of salvation becomes extremely fragile.** Many members believe they are saved by faith but also believe they lose their assurance of salvation every time they do the wrong thing and sin. They stay lost until they ask for forgiveness, then the discouraging process starts all over again.

B. **Matters of personal preference are viewed as sin.** Because the legalist's assurance is so dependent on correct behavior, his sin list is usually much too long. Various items get on the list that should simply be matters of personal preference and cultural conditioning. Little or no allowance is made for honest differences of interpretation and opinion. The legalist cannot understand how someone can be "saved" and still go canoeing on Sabbath. Purchasing gas on Sabbath when on a long journey for God is not a matter of personal preference to them; rather, it is breaking the Fourth Commandment. They say, "If you are violating my personal list, you are 'sinning' and must therefore have lost your hold on God."

C. **Victory is seen primarily as an outward event rather than an inner process.** Even if there are things on the sin list that the Scriptures do clearly prohibit, a legalistic person finds it hard to allow time for people's behavior to catch up with their hearts. They have difficulty understanding that a person may be undergoing enormous inner healing and change long before it shows up in outward behavior. Because their focus is outward, legalists think no change in behavior means no change at all and no connection with God.

D. **Externals dominate one's religious perspective.** Jesus said, "You blind fools and hypocrites. You strain a fly out of your drink and swallow a camel! You neglect the really important teachings of the law . . ." (Matthew 23:23, 24). We have to be very careful that we don't let matters of outward behavior get top billing instead of the deeper principles of justice, mercy, and love. When externals begin to dominate, the weightier matters of God's kingdom are undermined.

These four legalistic perspectives are poisonous to assurance of salvation. They keep people on edge spiritually. They create a judgmental atmosphere at church, in which well-meaning people carry around their sin lists trying to help others understand how to be more spiritual.

What a difference it makes to realize that Scripture focuses on who we are inside rather than what we do. Of course Scripture condemns certain behaviors, such as lying, stealing, murder, and adultery. The Bible condemns both sinful hearts and deeds, but one flows from the other. We commit sinful acts because of what is in our hearts. Jesus said, "From within, out of men's hearts, come evil thoughts, sexual immorality, slander, arrogance and folly. All these evils come from inside and make a man unclean" (Mark 7:20-23).

Salvation deals mainly with what George Knight labels the SIN behind the "sins" (George Knight, *I Used To Be Perfect*, p. 11). The fundamental SIN is alienation from God, not having a relationship with Him, living apart from Him. The Bible writers knew that once a person turns from being a rebel to being a lover, the main issue is settled. When the relationship is healed at conversion, the foundational SIN is also overcome, and we have salvation. The heart *is* the heart of the matter.

If we see sin in such relational terms, it becomes clear that healthy priorities and desires will eventually flow out of that new relationship with God.

> It is to the underlying state of brokenness [between us and Christ] that God primarily directs His saving grace, for if that alienation can be overcome and the separate united, the destructive coping behavior, the "sins," should become superfluous. Who will feel a compulsive urge to cover a guilt that no longer exists? Or who will need to prove his worth (materially or morally) to himself or to the neighbors (or to God) if the fact is not in question? Only what is in doubt has to be proved. Who will wish to escape from a fulfilled life? And who will cry out in loneliness and despair when wrapped in the gracious arms of His heavenly Father? Where there is no nakedness, neither will there be the need for fig-leaf aprons. (Jack Provonsha, *You Can Go Home Again,* p. 85)

We used to be estranged, now we are friends. That fundamental change in attitude and orientation is critical and enormously significant. When a young couple gets married, the vows are very simple, but who would question their huge implications? So it is between us and God.

The initial relationship with God may be feeble. Amidst our hurt and fear we may hardly be able to utter the cry for help. But God will hear. He will take that tiny beginning and build it into a deep bond of love. When we say Yes to God, an enormous number of heavenly "change agents" surge into our lives. The promise of Scripture is that once I surrender to God as best I know how, He instantly floods my life with mind-boggling heavenly resources. He tightens His grip. He moves in and starts shoveling out the garbage. God pours in the spiritual Miracle-Gro of love.

And the more we focus on deepening our relationship with God, the more profound the behavioral implications will be. If newlyweds are truly in love, do we really need to phone them on their honeymoon and remind them not to kill each other? Likewise, when we love God we will not want to hurt Him. The inner change is so fundamental that we'll feel like accident victims learning to walk all over again. It is a growth process that takes time, with ups and downs. Learning to love is infinitely more complex and significant than giving up Twinkies. But *during* that growth process, our salvation is secure. We study the marriage manual (Bible) not in order to see if we are married but to improve the marriage we already have. Such an emphasis not only provides the basis for assurance in Christ but also gives the Christian life a wonderfully joyful orientation.

Reflection

What do you wish God would do for you right now to strengthen your relationship with Him?

Shedding subtle legalism provides enormous help in solving what one author calls "Yo Yo Christianity," in which Christians feel they are saved one minute and lost the next. They ask for forgiveness in the morning and feel saved. Then they lose their temper or lust after a woman later and feel lost. But God doesn't operate that way.

Notice the following from the Spirit of Prophecy:

> We shall often have to bow down and weep at the feet of Jesus because of our shortcomings and mistakes, but we are not to be discouraged. Even if we are overcome by the enemy, we are not cast off, not forsaken and rejected by God. (*Steps to Christ,* p. 43)

When we fall on our spiritual faces we need to once again admit our need of forgiveness and continue to trust the Spirit's life-changing power. But that particular failure does not automatically cancel our salvation any more than a fight between a husband and wife automatically cancels their marriage. They need to reconcile their spat, to be sure, but the marriage does not end. As a preacher once said, "You may have dropped the soap but that doesn't necessarily mean you've stepped out of the shower." God looks at the trend of the life. Ellen White clearly states, "The character is revealed, not by occasional good deeds and occasional misdeeds, but by the tendency of the habitual words and acts" (*Steps To Christ*, p. 38). As long as the marriage is intact, salvation is intact. It does not help a marriage to be regularly asking, "Are we divorced today?" Two clear indications of the Spirit's work in our lives are (1) we feel a deepening sense of need and (2) Christ is becoming more precious and important to us (see *Steps to Christ*, p. 39, 44).

> It is my personal conviction that as long as we choose to keep our relationship with Jesus we retain our conversion during the time that victory is in process, before it is complete. I absolutely reject the on-off switch theory that justification turns salvation on and every subsequent sin turns it off until it is confessed, at which point justification turns it back on again. I believe that God accepts us with our character defects and the wrong behaviors that spring from them, as long as we maintain our relationship with Him. The way to turn off salvation is not by sinning, but by rebelling, by refusing even to be interested in salvation or in living the Christian life. Sadly, that is probably more often done by neglect than by choice. (Marvin Moore, *The Gospel vs Legalism,* p. 141)

> Christians are now a part of God's great covenant family and will remain so unless they subsequently choose to live a life characterized by rebellion against God. That is, they remain in God's family unless they choose SIN with a capital S and a capital I and a capital N—unless they choose SIN as a principle in their lives. (George Knight, *I Used To Be Perfect,* p. 42)

Reflection

What difference would it make in your Christian life if you could be as sure of your salvation now as you will be when you actually arrive in heaven?

Assurance Barrier #2: Distorted God-Concept

> Before anyone can really give his heart, soul, and mind to God, he must first know how much God has loved him, how God has thought about him from all eternity, and desired to share his life, joy, and love with him. Christian love is a response to God's infinite love, and there can be no response until one has somehow perceived that God has first loved him, so much so that he sent his only-begotten Son to be our salvation. (John Powell, *Why Am I Afraid to Love,* p. 10-11)

The gospel is primarily goods news about God. Unfortunately, many of us have re-made God in our own image, and our view is so distorted. We don't see things in life as they are, we see things as *we* are. Many people remain spiritually insecure because of the untrustworthy, distant God they have created in their own minds.

All the members of the Trinity are equally eager to accept and befriend us. They all love us equally. If the Father had been incarnated instead of Christ, He would have acted just the same. The Father and Christ are completely interchangeable, as is the Spirit. If you've seen One, you've seen them all. The truth is that the entire Trinity is far more interested in accepting you than you are in being accepted! They believe in you. They are rooting for you.

It is also true that the Trinity, in Their hearts, are already eager and willing to forgive you for every sin you might ever commit. Forgiveness is available long before you even ask. The Godhead has made full provision for your forgiveness through the life and death of Christ. The Scriptures teach that "while we were yet sinners, Christ died for us." The cross did not persuade God the Father to forgive; it simply revealed the forgiveness that was already in His heart from all eternity. That should dispel any notion that we have to "persuade" the Godhead to forgive. They already want to anyway. The only question is whether we will let them apply that forgiveness to our lives. The question has never been, "Does God *want* to forgive?" The only question is, "Will He *be able* to forgive?" That is determined by our willingness to admit our need and trust.

The vital importance of a healthy God-concept is brought out forcefully in the tragic story of Mike Gold:

> In the 1920s the philosopher of American communism was a Jew named Mike Gold. After communism fell into general disrepute in this country, Mike Gold became a man of oblivion. In this oblivion he wrote a book, *A Jew Without Knowing It.* In describing his childhood in New York City, he tells of his mother's instructions never to wander beyond four certain streets. She could not tell him that it was a Jewish ghetto. She could not tell him that he had the wrong kind of blood in his veins. Children do not understand prejudice. Prejudice is a poison that must gradually seep into a person's bloodstream.
>
> In his narration, Mike Gold tells of the day that curiosity lured him beyond the four streets, outside of his ghetto, and of how he was accosted by a group of older boys who asked him a puzzling question: "Hey, kid, are you a kike?" "I don't know," Mike said. He had never heard the word before. The older boys came back with a paraphrase of their question: "Are you a Christ-killer?" Again, the small boy responded, "I don't know." He had never heard that word either. So the older boys asked where he lived, and Mike, trained like most small boys to recite their address in the case of being lost, told them where he lived. "So you are a kike; you are a Christ-killer. Well, you're in Christian territory, and we are Christians. We're going to teach you to stay where you belong!" And so they beat the little boy, bloodied his face and tore his clothes, and sent him home to the jeering litany: "We are Christians and you killed Christ! Stay where you belong! We are Christians, and you killed Christ. . . ."
>
> When he arrived home, Mike Gold was asked by his frightened mother, "What happened to you, Mike?" He could answer only, "I don't know." "Who did this to you, Mike?" Again he answered, "I don't know." And so the mother washed the blood from the face of her boy and put him into fresh clothes and took him into her lap as she sat in a rocker and tried to soothe him. Mike Gold recalled much later in life that he raised his small, battered lips to the ear of his mother and asked, "Mama, who is Christ?"
>
> Mike Gold died in 1967. His last meals were taken at a Catholic Charity house in New York City, run by Dorothy Day. She once said of him, "Mike Gold eats every day at the table of Christ, but he will probably never accept him because of the day he first heard his name." And so he died. (John *Powell,Why Am I Afraid to Love,* p. 116)

In many ways, Mike Gold's experience is ours. So many of us have been beaten up by guilt for so many years that we cannot see God clearly. Our pews contain too many members who are near Christ but have never fully accepted Him. They may be singing in the choir but lack deep assurance of salvation because their own god is too remote or untrustworthy. A wrong God-concept can keep you at arm's length from joy.

Reflection

What has changed in your own concept of God during the past five years?

Assurance Barrier #3: Dependence on Feelings

After giving your life to Christ you may say, "But Kim, I don't feel any different. I don't feel saved." So what? Faith and feeling are as separate as Special-K loaf and ice cream. Suppose every time someone gave his life to Christ, an incredible surge of warm, tingly feelings gushed all over his being. Why would he need faith? The warm feeling would be evidence enough that he was saved.

Assurance of salvation has two main elements—Fact and Faith. A third element, warm feelings, may sometimes tag along. The sequence is critical. Think of a train as an analogy.

- Fact is the engine—God loves you and promises to save you.
- Faith is the passenger car—you trust that He has kept that promise in your life.
- Feeling is the caboose—you feel forgiven.

The key point is that even though it is nice to have a caboose on this particular train, it is not really necessary . Actually, feelings often run contrary to faith, and it is then that faith must rule. When feelings shout, "God is a million miles away" or "God won't forgive you," we are to choose to trust, no matter what our feelings say. Feelings can provide extremely helpful insights into our inner selves but cannot become the basis for our assurance of salvation.

Reflection

What do you think happens in our Christian experience when we put the caboose where the engine or passenger car should be? Has that ever happened to you?

Assurance Barrier #4: Worrying too much about You

Constantly second-guessing our assurance can hinder spiritual growth. Imagine a first-time gardener who goes out every morning, digs up his onion bulbs, and then buries them again. After one week of this his wife asks, "Charlie, what on earth are you doing out there?" "Oh," he replies, "I've been trying to see if my onions are growing, but I don't think this garden thing is working at all." She shouts back, "Are you crazy? Of course they won't grow if you keep checking!"

Ellen White gives some excellent counsel here:

> We should not make self the center and indulge anxiety and fear as to whether we shall be saved. All this turns the

> soul away from the Source of our strength. Commit the keeping of your soul to God, and trust in Him. Talk and think of Jesus. Let self be lost in Him. Put away all doubt, dismiss your fears. . . . Rest in God. He is able to keep that which you have committed to Him. If you will leave yourself in His hands, He will bring you off more than conqueror through Him that has loved you. (*Steps to Christ,* p. 49)

Reflection

If you could give away one spiritual worry you have about yourself, what would it be?

Assurance Barrier #5: Difficulty Trusting

Many people are so damaged by life's hurts that they find it difficult to trust anyone, including God. Someone who has suffered sexual abuse from her father will probably have a hard time trusting her heavenly Father. A man whose parents were alcoholics may have a difficult time believing that anyone really values him and that God will keep His promises. Prayer can be difficult for someone who has learned to stay closed up because of unresolved pain. People are often locked in self-destructive, self-protective behavior due to a lack of acceptance and love.

This is where the church can fulfill a vital role as the body of Christ. "Only the reassurance of an accepting and understanding love will lure the anxious, guilt-ridden and the supposedly inferior persons out from behind their defenses" (John Powell, *Why Am I Afraid To Love*, p. 54). "Never labor under the misconception that [your] acceptance breeds license. To the contrary, your very acceptance of a brother will make him strong" (Jerry Cook, *Love, Acceptance and Forgiveness*, p. 19). By the church modeling acceptance, the fearful one can say, "Oh, now I see what Christ's acceptance is all about. If Jesus is like you, I think I can trust Him for my salvation after all."

Review Questions

1. What was a memorable time someone forgave you for something you said or did? What insight can that provide into God's forgiveness?

2. What most often undermines your assurance of salvation?

3. How does this Spirit of Prophecy quote make you feel about God? "Those to whom He has forgiven most will love Him most, and will stand nearest to His throne to praise Him for His great love and infinite sacrifice" (*Steps To Christ,* p. 22).

Love in Action

My Choice:

Phone a friend or family member that you haven't called in quite a while and express your appreciation for him or her.

Your Choice:

Learning to be a Group: There are four levels of communication that are important to group life.

- Level 1: Cliches—"How is the weather?"
- Level 2: Reporting Facts—"My car broke down this week."
- Level 3: Ideas—"I really think small groups are important."
- Level 4: Feelings—"I feel discouraged today."

All levels are valuable, but we get to know and understand each other best on levels three and four.

Love in Action Feedback: How did the friend or family member react to your phone call?

Ice Breaker: "You are invisible for one day, what will you do?" (*Ice Breakers and Heart Warmers*, Steve Sheely, p. 56)

The Disciple's Heart

Have you ever had someone really believe in you? Did anyone ever give you the incredible gift of saying, "I think you are full of great potential. I have so much faith in you"? God says that to you every day. Often we cannot hear because we keep putting ourselves down. We have given up on ourselves. But the message is absolutely true nonetheless.

The sad fact is that too many Christians think less of themselves than God does. This lack of a personal sense of worth is poison to spiritual growth. God is your greatest fan. And because He loves you so deeply, He yearns to not only forgive but to recreate. He wants to deal not only with what sin has done to your past, but with what sin is doing to you now and will do in the future. As the Master Designer, He knows that human beings were created for fulfillment, peace, love, and joy.

The problem is that we often get God's intentions terribly garbled. When God offers us more than forgiveness, when He invites us to grow into happier living, we pigeonhole His offer and say, "Oh, I know what's going on here. We're right back to legalism and perfectionism again. We're right back to guilt and all those oppressive do's and don'ts." And the devil has fooled us and won.

> My father once adopted a beautiful black retriever dog from a nearby pound. The dog used to lie quietly in the corner of Dad's living room, eyeing him warily. One evening my father grabbed the daily paper to peruse the latest news. When he turned the page, the paper made a slight rattling sound, and the dog reacted by cowering behind a chair and shaking uncontrollably. It took Dad hours to calm him down with soothing words and gentle strokes. Only later did my father realize that the dog had been beaten repeatedly with a rolled up paper by its former owners and now reacted instinctively in anticipation of another round of abuse. Just that innocent rattling of a paper was too much for the anxious pup. It took months to convince the dog that he now had a real home, that he was not going to be thrown out, that he was loved. Later, that dog changed and followed Dad everywhere. They became inseparable.

That same kind of fear haunts many Adventists today whenever they hear the words "sanctification," "works," and "law." Many of us have been beaten up with guilt for so long that the slightest "rattling" of such words causes us to cower in spiritual self-protection. But properly understood, these are friendly words that point the way to a life of fulfillment. Rather than being painful reminders of our chronic inadequacies, these words should be promises of what God can do for us through His power.

> For a tiny seed tumbling around inside a seed package, the picture a glorious, full-grown tomato on the front of the seed package can be discouraging. All brown and shriveled, the seed feels inadequate. The picture is a painful reminder of its seedliness. "And you call yourself a tomato?" the devil taunts. The seed looks in the mirror and just hangs his head. But what if that seed could be convinced that the heavenly Gardener loves seeds? What if the seed could be convinced that it is the Gardener's job to turn seeds into tomatoes? Maybe that little seed could be coaxed out into the sunshine and trust enough to become all he was intended to be.

The truth is that sanctification is good news, just as justification is. For me to see sanctification as good news, however, I have to settle certain issues in my mind first.

1. That God is my friend and loves me unconditionally, just as I am.
2. That I have the assurance of salvation.
3. That everything I need to live the Christian life comes as a 100 percent gift from God.

Unless we nail down these three truths first, it is very dangerous to move on. But once we accept those truths, we are then able to safely examine the "S" word—sanctification—without feeling ill. Let's go slow. I promise not to rattle the paper too hard.

Reflection

Which of the three truths above do you wrestle with the most? Why?

Adventists seem fairly clear on the truth that we are justified by faith alone. The problem is that we often think we are then sanctified by faith and works. The truth is that we are also *sanctified* by *faith alone*.

- I have been crucified with Christ; it is no longer I who live, but Christ who lives in me; and the life I now live in the flesh I live by faith in the Son of God, who loved me and gave himself for me. (Galatians 2:20)
- As ye have received Christ Jesus [justification], so walk ye in Him [sanctification]. (Colossians 2:6)
- It is the grace of Christ alone, through faith, that can make us holy. (*Steps to Christ,* p. 40)
- By faith you became Christ's, and by faith you are to grow up in Him. (*Steps to Christ,* 47)
- This work [sanctification] can be accomplished only through faith in Christ, by the power of the indwelling Spirit of God. (*The Great Controversy,* p. 469)

In order for sanctification to be good news it must originate entirely from outside ourselves. Sanctification is a 100 percent gift because we are powerless to change the heart, where all true obedience occurs.

If justification is like getting married, sanctification is like staying married. Once you give your life to God, He immediately marshals all the resources of heaven to draw you ever closer to Himself and get rid of all that hinders your love relationship with Him and others. It is this ongoing, inner work of the Spirit that we call sanctification. Once you are justified, you automatically begin to grow spiritually. The faith relationship with Christ that was established at the time of your conversion connected you to the source of spiritual life. "Through this simple act of believing God [at conversion], the Holy Spirit has begotten a new life in your heart" (*Steps to Christ*, p. 34). New life is in you! Once you are connected to the power line, the lights are going to come on. Once you are pregnant, the baby will come.

Jesus said it so clearly: "Abide in me, and I in you. As the branch cannot bear fruit by itself, unless it abides in the vine, neither can you, unless you abide in me. He that abides in me, and I in him, he it is that bears much fruit, for apart from me you can do nothing" (John 15:4, 5).

What the behaviorist fails to remember is that it's what's going on *inside* that counts. To those who get nervous that the law will not be kept if we so fully depend on God, Ellen White poses this question: ". . . if the divine love is implanted in the soul, will not the law of God be carried out in the life?" (*Steps To Christ,* p. 40).

Haven't you noticed that the more a young man loves his girlfriend, the more anxious he is to please her in every itsy-bitsy detail? "Is there anything else I can do for you Linda, my darling?" he asks repeatedly. So it is in the spiritual realm. The more we emphasize love, the more we actually establish the law as a result. Wasn't it Paul who confidently declared, "For *all* the law is fulfilled in one word, even in this, Thou shalt love thy neighbor as thyself" (Galatians 5:14). Right behavior flows from right relationships, not the other way around. That sequence is vital.

> One day a pastor and his wife were traveling home from a meeting outside their district. They decided to purchase sandwich ingredients at the first supermarket they saw and put them together in the car. "I think I'd like some mustard on my sandwich," the wife mentioned casually. "I haven't had mustard in years." Her husband shot back angrily, "What? You know that stuff's bad for you! Suppose someone sees us? What would they think?" She persisted. As hubby approached the checkout with his little jar of contraband, he cased the store, nervously looking this way and that for a familiar face. Back on the highway the wife slapped some mustard on her cheese sandwich and relished the old, familiar taste. He sniffed the aroma, grew jealous of her enjoyment, and sheepishly asked, "Hey, could you put a little of that stuff on my sandwich too?" When they had eaten their fill, the husband remarked, "Now what on earth are we going to do with this half-used jar? We can't keep it in the fridge. Let's wait until we get to a remote area, and I'll chuck it out the window when no one's looking." And so he did. Years later he told me of the incident with sadness. He said, "How could I have become so infected by a church's subculture of fear that I would treat a little jar of mustard as if it were cocaine?"

Reflection

> Forgetting for a moment the right or wrong of mustard, reflect on how the pastor's perspective and sense of proportion could have gotten so twisted. How can that be prevented?

Such a subculture of fear and insecurity is the sure result of what I call the "Howard Hughes School of Sanctification." Let me illustrate:

> Howard Hughes was a billionaire. He owned almost anything he desired. He also had a phobia about germs. His approach to health was to avoid germs at all costs. In his later years he rented an entire floor of a fancy hotel and secluded himself there to avoid contact with the germy masses. One day he thought, "My word, there must be a lot of germs coming in these

windows," so he had them nailed shut. On another day he reasoned, "My staff is coming in and out of this room regularly, and they must be loaded with germs," so he covered the door with hard plastic that had a doggy door at the bottom through which to pass food. Later he observed, "Hey, this food I get three times a day must be crawling with germs," so he stopped eating altogether. Within weeks he died as a shriveled, old prune.

Now suppose that instead of trying to be healthy by avoiding germs, Howard had taken an entirely different approach to health. Suppose he had focused, instead, on absorbing all the good things of life. Suppose he had taken into his life all the water, fruit, nuts, vegetables, fresh air, and sunshine possible? Suppose he had exercised daily and lived to bless others? My guess is that no germ would have had a chance. And what a different, more positive outcome there could have been.

Jesus spoke of the Howard Hughes approach to sanctification in Matthew 12:43-45 when He talked about the man who cast out one evil spirit but left a vacuum for seven more to move in. Likewise, we can follow Howard's approach to spiritual health by focusing primarily on avoiding sin (germs), getting rid of sin, and become shriveled old Pharisees. Or we can focus on Jesus' approach, drinking in all the good things of heaven. Selfishness won't have a chance. One approach leads to anxiety and fear. The other leads to confidence and joy. One approach creates people who think it is their God-given mission to root sin out of the church. The other creates warm, generous hearts. One approach leads to a fortress mentality. The other engages the world with hands turned outward to serve.

> The plants and flowers grow not by their own care or anxiety or effort, but by receiving that which God has furnished to minister to their life. The child cannot, by any anxiety or power of its own, add to its stature. No more can you, by anxiety of effort of yourself, secure spiritual growth. The plant, the child, grows by receiving from its surroundings that which ministers to its life—air, sunshine, and food. What these gifts of nature are to animal and plant, such is Christ to those who trust in Him. (*Steps to Christ,* p. 45, 46)

People often fail to accept that sanctification is by faith alone because they misunderstand what the law is really all about. As Alden Thompson helpfully points out in his book *Inspiration*, the Ten Commandments are not God's primary, ultimate law. As important as the Ten Commandments are, they are simply an application of a more fundamental law (*Inspiration*, Alden Thompson, p. 114). The Ten Commandments were given by God after sin to meet the needs of self-centered, sinful human beings. They are a stripped-down version of heaven's original law, shaped to the limited comprehension of sinners. The Ten Commandments were never designed to be thought of as universal, eternal commandments for the entire universe for all time. How can angels commit adultery (they never marry)? How can angels honor their father and mother (they don't have parents)?

Ellen White writes,

> The LAW of God existed before man was created. The angels were governed by it. Satan fell because he transgressed the principles of God's government. . . . The principles of the ten commandments existed before the fall, and were of a character suited to the condition of a holy order of beings. After the fall, the principles of those precepts were not changed, but additional precepts [Ten Commandments, etc.] were given to meet man in his fallen state. (*3 Spiritual Gifts*, p. 295, emphasis supplied)

Ellen White says the principles behind the Ten Commandments existed before the fall and that those principles gave birth to additional precepts that were added after the fall. She points to a higher law on which the commandments were based. Jesus spoke of that law in the Sermon on the Mount when He said, "You have heard of old. . . . But I say unto you" (Matthew 5:21, 22). In Matthew 22:37-40 Jesus sums up all the Bible laws and boils them down to just two—(1) love God and (2) love your neighbor.

The Apostle Paul goes a step farther and combines these two into just one: "Therefore love is the fulfilling of the law" (Romans 13:10). The law underneath all other Scripture laws is love. That is the law that governs heaven. God wants this law to govern the entire universe, including us today. That law, that way of being and living, is the sum total of who God is Himself. "He who does not love does not know God; for God is love" (1 John 4:8).

This is why the Apostle Paul can say, "If I have prophetic powers and understand all mysteries and all knowledge . . . but have not love, I gain nothing" (1 Corinthians 13:1-3). A loving pork eater is more spiritual than an unloving vegetarian. A loving Sundaykeeper is far more spiritual than an unloving Sabbathkeeper.

Sanctification means becoming more loving. It deals more with the "why" of life than the "what." It focuses more on our motives than on specific actions. Outward obedience done from a self-centered motive is disobedience. Our motives reside in a safe-deposit box deep in our hearts, and only God has the key.

We now see clearly why sanctification must be by faith alone. I may be able to outwardly keep a bunch of "Thou Shalt Nots." I can use my willpower not to lie or steal. But once I understand the claims of God's law of love, I realize that such love is humanly impossible to manufacture. I cannot change my inside, from which love originates.

Reflection

What kind of people do you find the most difficult to love? How has God helped you grow in that area of your life?

Come to Golgotha and watch the murder of Christ. Clusters of flies buzz around Jesus' gaping wounds and crawl busily over the blood and spit that soak his beard. Rivulets of blood flow over our Lord's ears, neck, and face from the thorn punctures that ring his scalp. The punches and slaps from the soldiers at His trials have swollen his eyes nearly shut and raised black and blue welts on His cheeks and forehead. The lips are parched and blistered. His back has been laid open from two separate, nightmarish encounters with the thirty-nine lashes of the scourge. Blood streams down his torso and legs. The knees and elbows show long scrapes from being dragged across jagged pavement by the mobs. The spikes grate on hypersensitive nerve endings and send surges of pain shooting through His system. Taunts, ridicule, and mockery pour from the enthusiastic crowd.

Once that image has burned itself into our minds, we then need to ponder reverently this staggering Spirit of Prophecy quote:

> Although He [Christ] had the most fearful conflict with the powers of darkness, yet, amid it all, His love grew stronger and stronger. (*Testimonies,* vol. 2, p. 212)

Did you catch the last few words—"grew stronger and stronger"? If I had suffered the fearful, unjustified abuse that Christ endured from Gethsemane to the cross, I would feel I had gained a significant spiritual victory even if I became just a little upset. I would consider it an absolute miracle if, after such an ordeal, my love for my tormentors remained the same. But for my love for those thugs to grow stronger and stronger during such an experience is unthinkable. That kind of response is beyond anything I have ever seen or experienced. And yet that's exactly what was going on in Jesus' heart. He loved them more afterward than He did before.

When it comes to defining the love of God, the "grew stronger" love that Jesus expressed on the cross is the only true standard. And it is that kind of love that God wants to pour into our lives each day. Those big religious words such as "perfection," "sanctification," "holiness," and "righteousness" all boil down to love.

Unfortunately our bankrupt human hearts can only, at best, love conditionally. We say, "I'll love you if . . ." or "I love you because. . . ." We set conditions.

> Suppose we look in for a moment on a typical wedding. The minister asks the beaming bride, "Julie, do you take Fred here to be your lawfully wedded husband, to have and to hold in sickness and in health . . . ?" All the congregation hears is Julie's sweet, sincere reply, "I do." But if we could somehow look inside Julie's brain when the minister is asking that question, we would probably hear her thinking, *Yes, I do, if he comes home on time, if he buys me new clothes each month, if he obeys my mother, if he keeps a good job, if . . . if . . . if. . . .* And when Fred doesn't live up to her expectations, her love is withdrawn in some way.
>
> Then there is the "because" kind of love. We humans usually relish this type of love. Suppose a wife asks her husband, "Why do you love me, my darling?" He replies, "Oh, I love you because you are so pretty, because you are such a good mother, because you cook such delicious meals, because. . . because. . . ." She will be all smiles and feel glowy inside. But suppose she later gets in a severe car accident and her face is scarred. Suppose she one day massacres an important supper for hubby's boss. Hubby typically withdraws his love and gets upset.

Both "if" and "because" kinds of love have conditions and therefore create insecurity in the other person. They are nothing but human counterfeits.

All love that originates in our human hearts is just selfishness in disguise. People can treat others kindly because they want something in return:

- affection
- recognition
- security
- a good reputation
- friendship
- baptisms.

Yes, baptisms. Even our attempts at witnessing can have selfish motives. We may witness in order to prove we are right or to win praise and commendation or to "see our church grow."

We may have sincerely thought we were pretty caring ("Not perfect, but better than a lot of people") until Jesus came along and demonstrated an unconditional love that is truly mind-boggling. God loves us not because we are handsome, talented, or bright. He loves us because *He is Love*. It is His very nature to love, just as it is a rose's nature to bloom. We cannot earn His love, nor can we turn it off. Ellen White even indicates that God's love is so strong, so intense, that we have to actively resist it in order to be lost (*Steps to Christ*, p. 27).

Reflection

Tell about a time when God's love became especially real for you.

The very real challenge we now face, however, is to discover how we can reproduce God's love in our own hearts as disciples. God might as well have asked me to jump to the moon. There's simply no way. In fact, that's exactly where I need to begin. I first need to see that my own pitiful attempts at love are simply selfishness dressed up in fancy clothes. Then the Holy Spirit can begin to change me from the inside out.

Suppose we made two lists. List A is all the things in the Christian life that God produces. List B is all the things in the Christian life that we produce on our own.

List A—What God produces	**List B—What we produce on our own**
• Interest in spiritual things	•
• Willingness to be changed	•
• Hope	•
• Repentance	•
• Faith	•
• Forgiveness	•
• Sanctification	•
• Love	•
• A sense of need for prayer	•
• A sense of need to read Scripture	•
• Understanding our worth	•
• Willingness to forgive others	•

OK now, let's compare the two lists. How did we do? Oh my, List B isn't very long. In fact, it adds up to exactly zero. And God's list is only the beginning; we could add a zillion more things. It is all a gift, you see. The Christian life is based on God's grace from start to finish.

> Imagine a little caterpillar looking up at a gorgeous butterfly and then down at himself and saying, "No way, man, it can never happen to me. For one thing, I don't have a clue how to fly. How am I supposed to afford flying lessons on my meager salary? And how will I ever overcome my fear of heights? I don't even see the beginnings of a wing on either side of my furry body, not even a stub. And those colors! How on earth can this drab torso ever get to be so colorful? It's just not me. And such grace! Look how that butterfly glides along the air currents so effortlessly and lands delicately on the branches. All I can do is clunk along. I just don't see how any of it can happen to me at all." Then one day the caterpillar decides to trust. He trusts enough to spin a cocoon, just like mother instructed, and be patient. And within a few days—presto!—he has his very own personal miracle to write home about (just as soon as he comes down from doing ecstatic loops and flips above the trees).

How did such a transformation happen? What was the caterpillar's part? To trust and ask God to take control. What was God's part? To keep His promise and create something new. The Apostle Paul put it this way:

> Therefore if any man be in Christ, he is a new creature: old things are passed away; behold, all things are become new. (2 Corinthians 5:17)

> For we are his workmanship, created in Christ Jesus unto good works, which God hath before ordained that we should walk in them. (Ephesians 2:10)

> For it is God which worketh in you both to will and to do of his good pleasure. (Philippians 2:13)

Notice that it is even up to God to create within us the will or desire. All we have to do is be willing to be made willing. Ellen White has observed, "You cannot atone for your past sins; you cannot change your heart and make yourself holy. But God promises to do all this for you through Christ" (*Steps To Christ*, p. 33).

God's goal is to equip you, by His Spirit, to be the kind of person who can both receive love and give it. His Spirit arranges circumstances and situations in our life to accomplish His purposes. He is working 24 hours a day to make you loving and trusting. At times it may seem like you are going in reverse, but you must continue to trust. God will make it as difficult as possible for you to give up. And if you let Him, God will not stop until you are an open, accepting, transparent, secure, trusting, victorious disciple of Christ.

Reflection

The main reason people are afraid to really be open and be themselves around others is: (choose one and explain)

a. Lack of confidentiality
b. Fear of rejection
c. Don't like themselves
d. Lack of confidence
e. Other ____________

Jeremiah talks about reaching a level of Christian maturity where God writes the principles of love so deeply within our hearts that we are no longer motivated by a checklist but simply live love unconsciously (Jeremiah 31:33-34). That is how "by beholding we become changed" (2 Corinthians 3:18). We become so enamored with Christ that more and more of His life naturally becomes ours through His Spirit. That is similar to what happens to the cellist who has so internalized the music that it simply flows through his fingers—he doesn't even need to look at the notes.

Following that theme, Ellen White makes the following statement:

> All true obedience comes from the heart. It was heart work with Christ. And if we consent, He will so identify himself with our thoughts and aims, so blend our hearts and minds into conformity to His will, that when obeying him we shall be but carrying out our own impulses. The will, refined and sanctified, will find its highest delight in doing His service. When we know God as it is our privilege to know Him, our life will be a life of continual obedience. Through an appreciation of the character of Christ, through communion with God, sin will become hateful to us. (*The Desire of Ages,* p. 668)

At this point you might be thinking, "If the Christian life depends so much on God, what then is the place of human effort? Am I just a passive rag doll?" Hardly. Human effort for the Christian is living out what God puts in. God implants new dreams, desires, and love in our hearts, then He depends on us, in His strength, to carry them out. For instance, my daughter loves to make music, but her oboe doesn't play itself. She must move her fingers and practice. A friend of mine loves mountain climbing, and in order see the view from the top, he must move his legs and sweat. Another friend loves teaching children and spends endless hours preparing lesson plans. A mother loves her child and makes an incredible investment of time and money in the little one's development. None of these people's works are artificial. We would call their efforts a "labor of love" that originates from deep within. Because of that combination of inner love and outward effort, their music, mountain climbing, teaching, and mothering all bring them enormous satisfaction. They are simply expressing the love that is already there. They are "carrying out their own impulses." So it is in the Christian life. Because God gave me a love for sharing His good news, I spend long hours at night writing Bible lessons like these. It is hard work, and I don't always feel like doing it, but I love to do it. Indeed, I would be frustrated if I could not express my inner desires in that way.

Christian works also safeguard and develop the trust relationship with God that is at the foundation of the Christian life. As the Spirit creates a desire to know Christ, that relationship will become a greater and greater priority. Because our trust relationship with God is so vital, we need to take seriously those things that He says *enhance* that relationship and those things that tend to *destroy* it. In any marriage, there are activities that enhance the marriage and those that weaken it. So it is in our marriage to God.

Relationship Enhancers

The most important faith enhancer is communication. Because God is the most trustworthy Person in the universe, the more we know Him, the more we will love and trust Him. Another vital relationship enhancer is cooperation with the Spirit. Every time we cooperate with Him by following through on the desires He implants within our hearts, it makes it easier for Him to strengthen our dependence on Him. Serving others also deepens our closeness to Him. In order for this relationship to become top priority, the Spirit promises to "crucify" the old preferences and desires that pull us away (Galatians 2:20). The Spirit also makes clear the true meaning of lordship, where Jesus becomes the ultimate authority in our lives.

Relationship Destroyers

There are also things in life that erode our trust relationship with Christ. Whenever we resist or stifle the work of the Spirit in our hearts by ignoring Him or saying, "No," we hinder Him. Sin is bad news not primarily because we have done "naughty things" but because we are putting holes in our own boat. We are strengthening the part of our brain that resists God and says, "God is the enemy!" We are injuring the trust that is the basis of our relationship with Christ (*Steps to Christ*, p. 20). If we keep that up long enough, we can, over time, stop trusting altogether, rebel, and have a spiritual divorce. That would surely break God's heart again.

That's why God says, "I accept you, but you have to allow Me to do something about those relationship destroyers or else they could eventually take you from Me."

In summary, bad works are those by which we try to earn salvation out of our own selfish motives. Good works are those that grow out of the new life, motives, and priorities that the Holy Spirit implants within our hearts.

Finally, we need to realize that we are just as dependent on God to keep us saved as we were to become saved in the first place. The issue is not how well we can hang onto God, but how able He is to hang onto us.

> Suppose my daughter was two years old again and we had to cross a busy city street. Cars, trucks, buses, vans, and motorcycles are whizzing by, honking, screeching, squealing. From her perspective the vehicles seem huge. The noise is frightening. She can't even read the signal that tells you when to walk. From the sidewalk she stares wide-eyed at the road so full of potential disaster. To her the other side seems miles away. She reaches up her sweaty little hand, and I grasp it tightly in mine. She yields control and trusts.
>
> Do you think it ever crosses her mind that her safety depends on the strength of her grip? Believe me, if that's what she

> thought, she would never budge off that curb. Once she reaches up her hand, it is up to me to make sure she makes it across safely. We make it because my hand is strong, not hers. Nothing would ever get me to let go in the middle of that street, nothing! In fact, if I did intentionally let go partway across, I could be accused of child abuse. And if that makes so much sense in our human relationships, why can't it make much more sense in our relationship to God?

Jesus told us, "My Father . . . is greater than all, and no one is able to snatch [you] out of the Father's hand" (John 10:29). Ellen White wrote, "Let us keep our eyes fixed upon Christ and He will preserve us. Looking unto Jesus we are safe. Nothing can pluck us out of His hand" (*Steps to Christ*, p. 49). Again she counsels, "If you will leave yourself in His hands, He will bring you off more than conqueror through Him that has loved you" (*Steps To Christ*, p. 49).

Review Questions

1. Tell about a time that you genuinely felt loved unconditionally. Can you relate that experience to God's love?

2. How can we teach high standards and yet make sure that people, especially children and teenagers, fully sense the unconditional nature of God's love?

3. "If I could count on the prayer support of this study group, I would like to begin trusting God more fully in. . . ." (finish the sentence)

Love in Action—Important!

My Choice:

Bring fruit to the next group meeting when you study "The Telescope." Someone should also bring a basket to make a group fruit basket. Have a group member take it to a shut-in or homeless shelter after the meeting.

Your Choice:

Learning to be a Group: It is helpful to keep the conversation on the subject at hand rather than taking too many sidetracks and "chasing too many rabbits."

Love in Action Feedback: Collect all the fruit tonight and make up a group fruit basket. Choose someone to deliver it to a shut-in or homeless shelter this coming week.

Ice Breaker: What is one of your greatest fears? Why? What helps you cope?

The Telescope

Imagine an astronomer who has no telescope and has never even heard of one. His only source of information about the heavens is personal observation with the unaided eye. Because his view is so limited, he has been able to glean very little insight into the workings of the universe above. "Oh, if I only could see farther!" he moans. One day a large package arrives for his birthday. He eagerly opens the gift and finds inside a large item with the label on its side, "Precision Telescope." No one bothered to include instructions, however. He has never seen anything like it before—so sleek, so shiny, so intricately made. He takes it out carefully and puts the telescope in a prominent place on his mantle. There it sits for years. He polishes it regularly and shows it to admiring friends. He is sure that this is the best "telescope" ever made. Never does it occur to him to stop looking at it and start looking through it. Years later you can still see him out in his back yard at night, squinting up at the heavens and lamenting his limited vision of the stars. He has made the tragic mistake of viewing the telescope as an end in itself, not a means to an end.

"What a silly man," you might say. But many Adventists are inadvertently doing the same thing every day with their beliefs. The doctrines of the Adventist church are intricate, shiny, and well put together. They are priceless gifts of truth. They are biblically sound and correct. But have you ever asked the question, "Why did God give them? Why is it important to believe as we do?"

Unless the answer to those questions is clear, we can easily become like the hapless astronomer. We can wind up making the doctrines an end in themselves rather than a means to an end. The key is to take the doctrines down from the mantel and look through them to see God. The more fully we comprehend His love, the more fully the Spirit can enable us to reflect that love to others. It is by beholding that we are changed (2 Corinthians 3:18).

One evening I was scheduled to begin a new Bible study with a lovely non-Adventist family of four. As pastor of the church, I chose to take along one of my well-grounded church members for training. All went well for the first five sessions. After the sixth lesson, the wife retreated to her kitchen and returned with a tray full of homemade cakes and four cups of coffee. She had obviously spent considerable time preparing these refreshments as a token of her appreciation for the wonderful truths she was learning. When my fellow church member spied the coffee, he immediately launched into a detailed lecture on the evils of caffeine. The wife's smile turned to a look of horror at having committed such a dreadful blunder, and she soon slunk back to her kitchen, ashamed. When we returned to the car, I brimmed with what could barely be called righteous indignation. "Don't ever act that way again. You're timing is awful," I fumed. "But I was just trying to witness for the truth," he replied. I

> then felt bad that as pastor I had apparently failed to make it clear that people are more important than information.
>
> Later that evening I lay awake in bed wondering, "Where could this normally pleasant Adventist have gotten the idea that it is OK to stomp all over someone's emotions in order to uphold truth? How had a church member become so knowledgeable about Bible facts and so ignorant about love?" I finally concluded that he too had put the telescope up on the mantel to be admired. He too believed the doctrines, accepted them all, but never understood their deeper meaning and purpose. How tragic.

During the late 1800s many Adventists failed to comprehend the importance of a personal relationship with God and preached our distinctive doctrines *without* emphasizing the need to know Christ. Mrs. White commented that we were "as dry as the hills of Gilboa." There were remnants of that problem even when I became a theology major in college (and that was definitely quite a ways into this century!).

> During 1969 and 1970, revival burned its way across Seventh-day Adventist college campuses. Jesus' love and unlimited grace became frequent topics of discussion in dorm lobbies and over lunch. Prayer bands formed spontaneously at all hours of the day and night. Many students, including theology majors, found the message of righteousness by faith for the first time. Looking back at that soul-stirring experience, the question haunts me still, "How could so many Seventh-day Adventist young people, even student leaders, have known so much about doctrine but so little about Christ?"

Thankfully we are making significant progress in realizing that a relationship with God is vital. Today, however, most teaching about a relationship with Christ views this relationship as an *addition to* our distinctive doctrines. We somehow believe we have captured the proper emphasis by teaching about a relationship with Jesus first and then talking about doctrines. Because of this unnecessary separation, we are seeing the development within Adventism of two camps. One camp feels the need to give great prominence to our distinctive doctrines. The other camp feels the need to emphasize relationships. Such a dichotomy is both frustrating and unnecessary.

It is now time to further our understanding and discover the full potential of our teachings. It is time we understand how to have a relationship with God *through* our distinctive doctrines. Through the doctrines we see God more clearly. Through the doctrines we are able to develop a deeper relationship with Christ.

The marriage of doctrines and relationships is not new. Jesus married these two concepts when He said, "You shall know the truth and the truth shall make you free!" The truth will free you from destructive, childish, inappropriate ways of relating to God and others.

Jesus also said,

> Thou shalt love the Lord thy God with all thy heart, and with all thy soul, and with all thy mind. This is the first and great commandment. And the second is like unto it. Thou shalt love thy neighbour as thyself. On these two commandments hang all the law and the prophets. (Matthew 22:36-40)

Isn't that wonderful? The Scriptures were not an end in themselves but the means to a much larger purpose. Jesus taught that if you take all that has been written from Genesis to Malachi, it all has one supreme purpose—to enable us to love.

The Apostle Paul also married doctrines and relationships when he said, "And though I . . . understand all mysteries, and *all knowledge* . . . and have not [love] I am *nothing*" (1 Corinthians 13:2). Frankly, I shudder every time I read that quote.

> Imagine meeting someone who knows everything there is to know. This person has a great answer for every spiritual issue you might raise. He can bring forth quote after quote to support his views. He speaks forcefully and is charismatic in his appearance and demeanor. Let's face it, most of us would be very impressed. So we ask the Apostle Paul for his assessment. "Paul, what do you think? Pretty knowledgeable guy, wouldn't you say?" Paul turns with that special look of wisdom that comes from someone who has really experienced God and says, "That man is nothing! He is a fact-laden zero." Imagine . . . zero. What is the problem? A lack of love.

Reflection

Which of the following two churches do you think is more pleasing to God and why?

1. *Antarctica Church* teaches no biblical error at all. All of its doctrines are correct. The only problem is that the church membership is split down the middle over some peripheral issue. One half is not talking to the other half. The atmosphere is cold. Brrr!

2. *Bahama Church* teaches baptism by sprinkling, worships on Sunday, and is all mixed up on the end-time prophecies, but has taken Jesus' call to love very seriously and demonstrates that love day in and day out. The church membership is united and is a source of help and wholeness for hundreds of people in the community. The atmosphere is warm and accepting.

At this point I can hear someone asking, "So, just as long as we feel lovey-dovey, it doesn't make any difference what we believe?" No, that's not what I'm saying at all. In fact, there are several good reasons why it is very important to hold on to right doctrine and not simply attend whatever church happens to feel the most loving. There are strong reasons to "hang in there" in an Antarctica Church when you could be sunning yourself in a balmy Bahama Church. Some of those reasons are:

1. Right scriptural teachings enable us to form the most complete concept of God.
2. Correct biblical teachings give the fullest picture of what true love is all about.
3. The church with the most truth has the greatest potential for being the most loving.

Nonetheless, God is still most interested in what kind of people all our knowledge is making us. If we know all the Adventist truths and have memorized all sixty–six books of the Bible but are frequently

- Harsh
- Opinionated
- Critical
- Negative
- Argumentative
- Independent
- Stubborn or
- Judgmental

then we've most likely missed the point.

That's how you wind up with church members who are factual giants but experiential pygmies. Members who are doctrinal geniuses and relational dummies. Once you have looked through the telescope and seen the incredible glories beyond, you can no longer be satisfied with debating and arguing over some piece of the telescope stand or lens adjuster.

Perhaps you have read the following Spirit of Prophecy quote: (read it again, slowly)

> Of all the people in the world, reformers should be the most unselfish, the most kind, the most courteous. (*Gospel Workers,* 1915, p. 507)

Let's explore that quote. Who would be your choice for the most unselfish person in the world? As you survey every country around the globe, who would turn out to be the kindest individual? And the most courteous? "Courteous" is defined in the dictionary as being "characterized by graciousness . . . consideration toward and respect for others" (*American Heritage Dictionary*, 2nd ed.). And Mrs. White says reformers should be like that. Wow! Reformers are supposed to be such wonderful people. Why is it that they are the kindest? Because they have the greatest insight into the teachings of the Word, the doctrines. The greater our understanding of truth, the kinder we should be. The better we know doctrine, the better we should know God. That relationship, in turn, enables the Spirit to make us more like Him.

One of the clearest indications that someone is only a false reformer is when they are harsh, stubborn, domineering, or pushy. Such self-appointed reformers may know a lot of facts, but they have never mastered the purpose for those facts. "They are the true disciples of Christ, not who know the most, but who love the most" (Spanheim as quoted in *Who Cares About Love*, p. 30).

Reflection

Many people's theology grows out of their personality. Insecure people, for instance, may emphasize more of God's justice than His mercy. How do you feel your upbringing and personality have influenced how you relate to God?

Fred lived in a small poverty-stricken town "up north." As an unemployed factory worker, he had a lot of time on his hands. Trying to keep busy, Fred took time one day to clean out the attic of his 200-year-old home. While rummaging, he came across an old book and in it found an yellowed map. After bringing the aged map downstairs, he examined it carefully in the light of day. He recognized the name of a river that ran across one corner. He could also identify the name of a large hill in the center. "Why this area is only about one mile away!" he exclaimed. The markings, handwritten in an archaic style, included a date, 1868. Snaking through the map was a dotted line that ended at a large "X." Under the "X" were the carefully etched words, "Huge treasure right here."

Fred had seen old maps of that area before, and as he carefully studied this one, he became convinced that it was the only truly correct representation of the land and its varied features.

Fred showed his map to an unemployed friend who happened to have his own old map of the same area. Fred pointed out that the neighbor's map was actually incorrect. It had the river in the wrong place, and the hill was not even marked at all. Eventually convinced, the neighbor believed in Fred's map too. Fred then mailed out fliers to the community inviting them to come and learn about the map. Two middle-aged people responded and both also believed that the geographic features on Fred's map were remarkably accurate. Over the next several years a Map Club developed. To be a member you had to believe in the old map and pay $50 dues per year. All the members were glad and secure in the knowledge that Fred's map was absolutely correct.

> No one, however, asked why the map was written in the first place. No one ever inquired about the treasure to which it pointed. No one even thought about using the map to look for the treasure.
>
> The ancient map was correct but useless. Its original author had written and preserved it in vain. The map had become an end in itself rather than the means to an end—discovering treasure. Fred taught the truth, but his teaching was incomplete and therefore of little value to him or his club members. He may even have done considerable harm by inadvertently teaching the members to ignore the booty.

Like Fred's map, our doctrines all point the way to the treasure of a deeper relationship with God. But unless we teach and emphasize that larger purpose, we will have developed nothing more than a club of knowledgeable spiritual paupers. Whenever any of our doctrines is presented, it must give additional insight into the character of God and our relationship to Him and others. Otherwise, it is incomplete and, therefore, a distortion.

The doctrines are tools God has given us with which to build a relationship with Him. Tools can be used to build things or they can be left in the toolbox to be admired. Tools can also be used to tear down and destroy. The tools are not the house, they are the means for building the house.

Focusing on the Sabbath doctrine, Jesus commented, "The Sabbath was made for man, and not man for the Sabbath" (Mark 2:27). Isn't it obvious that people are more important than medicine, no matter how terrific that medicine is?

Because the doctrines are God's means to enable us to love Him and others, it is absurd to argue about the doctrines. That is why it is so tragic to split churches over doctrine. How can we talk in unloving ways about that which is designed to produce love? Isn't that a clear sign that we have missed some huge point somewhere?

The apostle Paul put it so beautifully:

> All scripture is given by inspiration of God, and is profitable for doctrine, for reproof, for correction, for instruction in righteousness: That the man of God may be perfect, thoroughly furnished unto all good works. (2 Timothy 3:16)

He also wrote this:

> But speak thou the things which become sound doctrine: That the aged men be sober, grave, temperate, sound in faith, in [love], in patience. The aged women likewise, that they be in behaviour as becometh holiness. . . . (Titus 2:1)

Paul says that God gave us sound doctrine for the purpose that we be enabled to do "good works" and become people of love and patience.

Note prayerfully how the Spirit of Prophecy links truth and life:

> The reason that the Lord can do so little for those who are handling weighty truths is that so many hold these truths apart from their life. (Manuscript Release, vol. 15, MS 1141, p. 21)
>
> . . . we shall force them to the conclusion that the doctrine we profess cannot be the Christian doctrine, since it does not make us kind, courteous, and respectful. (*Counsels to Writers and Editors,* p. 71)

Reflection

> You are on a plane traveling to visit a relative. You strike up a conversation about religion with the divorced lady next to you. She is all aglow about her church. The church has changed her life and become her lifeline of love. Pretend you're convinced that God wants you to help her see that the Seventh-day Adventist Church is what she ultimately needs. What do you say?

Each of the doctrines is like a different color of paint with which to create a wonderful picture of God. It is the purpose of God that our end-time picture of Him be the clearest and most compelling since Apostolic times. The remnant church's most distinguishing characteristic is its access to the fullest spectrum of color with which to portray God.

> Suppose we use the analogy of "paint by the numbers." Each number in the picture represents a different shade. Centuries ago, after the New Testament church passed off the scene, the Christian church began to omit certain key colors from the palette of truth. By the Middle Ages, only dark, foreboding hues remained. These dreary colors were substituted for the originals, and the picture of God became dramatically distorted.

Gradually, over the centuries, the colors have been rediscovered one by one:

- Righteousness by faith
- Priesthood of all believers
- Baptism by immersion
- The Ten Commandments
- The Sabbath
- The sanctuary
- The state of the dead
- The Second Coming

> Up until the formation of the Seventh-day Adventist church, some colors were still undiscovered and distortions continued. Eternally burning hell and the immortality of the soul, for instance, painted a horrible picture of God. Now the palette is restored, and we have been given the enormous privilege of revealing God's portrait to the world.
>
> How sad if we never use the colors for their intended purpose. How tragic if we simply call attention to the colors themselves—their brilliance, texture, and purity. How tragic if the colors become ends in themselves instead of the means to an end. If that happens, we are able to paint no clearer a picture of God than other Protestant churches. Colors left on the palette are no better than no colors at all.

Over the years I have asked many Adventists what they think our message to the world is. I wanted to find out what they think our church was called into existence to proclaim. The most common answers I get are:

- The Sabbath
- The Second Coming
- The judgement
- The mark of the beast

Is there anything wrong with these answers? Yes! They're incomplete. They miss the big picture. The Apostle John didn't miss it when he opened the three angels' messages with the foundational truth, "Fear God and give glory to Him . . ." (Revelation 14:7). Ellen White didn't miss it when she wrote, "The last rays of merciful light, the last message of mercy to be given to the world, is a revelation of His character of love" (*Christ's Object Lessons*, p. 415). Again we see that our last-day message of instruction and warning is ultimately designed to enhance people's understanding of God. People who have missed it say things such as, "We now have 1,000 Sabbathkeepers in that country." Is that the big picture, to make "Sabbathkeepers" out of everyone? As vital as Sabbath is, if it becomes our primary focus rather than God, we have inadvertently created an idol that even God can't endorse.

Imagine a story about a lonely girl who has lost her lover and cannot find him. Suppose I discover where the lover lives and that he wants to meet with the girl every Saturday at the park. There is danger in this story, however. The bridge on the road to the park has been washed out by a violent storm. I run to the girl and say, "You must go to the park every Saturday, not Sunday, but Saturday, and be very careful because the bridge has been washed away!" Did I deliver the message correctly? I got the day and warning correct. What's the problem? *I didn't talk about the lover.* We cannot allow ourselves to simply become specialists in days and washed out bridges.

Reflection

What is your favorite doctrine and what has it meant in your life?

Now we come to the most crucial questions of all:

- How, then, do the doctrines reveal God?
- How do they help us understand how to relate to Him in love?

Here are a few rudimentary thought-starters for a few doctrines. You and the Holy Spirit can go much deeper.

Sabbath

The Sabbath was given as a day between lovers. It was created to help us get to know God.

But there is another purpose. The whole issue of which day on which to worship—Saturday or Sunday—teaches us vital lessons about how to relate to God. The Saturday/Sunday issue *defines* what our relationship to God will be like. Keeping Saturday rather than Sunday teaches us that God is to be the ultimate authority in our lives. I think we have to admit that outwardly one day of the week looks like any other. I haven't noticed that Saturdays are any sunnier, on average, than Sundays. The only thing that makes the days different is that God said so. He said it, I do it, and that settles it. He is the ultimate authority in my life. I do not relate to Him as an equal. I do not relate to Him on my own terms. I relate to Him as One who always knows what is best for my life. He is Lord.

Baptism by Immersion

When I go under the waters of baptism, I am burying self. When I come up out of the water, I am symbolically saying that I will live in total dependence on God for spiritual life. He is my Source. My new life as a Christian is not a 50:50 proposition. It is not even a 99:1 proposition. I am living spiritually 100 percent because of God. I am as dependent on Him for spiritual growth as a dead corpse is to be resurrected. Sprinkling does not portray that truth. Sprinkling conveys the wrong message about dependence on God.

The Millennium

The Millennium teaches us much about the character of God. God does not say to the redeemed saints, "Hey, I'm the boss around here. I don't want anyone questioning my decisions as to who gets into heaven and who does not." Instead, God says, "Look, I'll throw open all the records, all the books, and I'll give you 1,000 years to ask any questions you want." God is not secretive. He is eminently fair, considerate, and trustworthy.

State of the Dead

The truth that the dead cannot communicate with us safeguards our relationship with God against false communication. The basis for any in-depth relationship is accurate information, and our doctrine of the state of the dead keeps the channels of communication pure by cutting off any possibility that the devil will impersonate departed loved ones and give us erroneous information about God.

Health Message

The only way for God to communicate with us is through our brains. If we are to have an effective relationship with Him, then those communication channels need to be as clear as possible. Our health message is not primarily designed to help us live longer; it is mainly designed to keep our minds fully open to receive messages from God's Word and the Spirit. The clearer the communication, the deeper our response of love.

Heavenly Sanctuary

A key message from the heavenly sanctuary is that Christ can cleanse our soul temple from all that interferes with our relationship to Him. Selfishness is an enormous barrier to love. It shuts us off from God. Jesus' sanctuary ministry makes available to us all the resources of heaven to rid us of selfishness and sin. Do you remember when Jesus cleansed the temple here on earth? The area of the temple from which He chased the money changers and cattle was the court of the Gentiles. With all that noise and chaos, the Gentiles could not come close to Him in worship. Therefore, Christ did that which they could not do for themselves, and He got rid of every barrier between Himself and the Gentile worshipers. Now, from heaven, He wants to do the same for the temple of our hearts. He clears away the rubbish of self, clears away everything that hinders love.

What a marvelous God our doctrines reveal! He loves us so much that He has taken the initiative in establishing, developing, and maintaining a deep love relationship with each of us.

- He seeks us out,
- He attracts us to Himself by explaining who He is,
- He chooses a special day to spend together,
- He safeguards our relationship,
- He removes the barriers.

Each of the doctrines is like a different window into the heart of God. Once we see that ultimate truth, it becomes plain how, as Ellen White says, "Christ is the center of all true doctrine" (*Counsels to Parents & Teachers*, p. 453).

Review Question

Explain how the following doctrines do the following:

1. Help us understand what God is like and/or

2. Help us understand how to relate to Him in love

Doctrine

Second Coming:

Judgment:

Tithing:

Learning to be a Group: It is helpful if discussion flows between group members rather than always being directed back to the group leader. Build on each other's comments. Help to gently draw each other into the discussion.

Love in Action Feedback: How did the recipients of the fruit basket react?

Group Activity: Matching Squares.

Lovesharing

The words "evangelism" and "witnessing" are so misunderstood that those two words ought to be discarded. Evangelism usually conjures up mental images of public meetings where the pastor, or some outside preacher, explains our doctrines to non-Adventists. Witnessing has so often been connected with door-to-door visitation and asking unsuspecting strangers if they know Jesus, that the mere mention of the word makes many members break out in a cold sweat. These definitions are far too narrow. It is like describing the word "color" by holding up just an orange card. Such limitations lead to distortions.

I'm convinced that trying to explain the old terms is hopeless. We need to start over from the ground up. We need to discover a replacement word, fresh and open to all the colors of the biblical spectrum. To help focus our thinking in a new direction, I'm going to use a new word—lovesharing—to describe all contacts with non-Adventists. Let's discover together what lovesharing is all about.

Information And Relationships

Lovesharing gives priority to relationships. Recently a pastor told me the following story:

> As a young, devout Catholic, Maria attended mass with her three little girls every morning. Maria had never even heard of a Seventh-day Adventist, but she came to our group Bible study out of curiosity after a group member urged, "You've just got to hear about the mark of the beast!" I earnestly wanted to change the subject of that study, but everyone insisted we proceed. And so, with a silent prayer to the Holy Spirit for wisdom and tact, I launched into the subject as carefully as possible.
>
> At the end of the study on the beast, very-Catholic Maria looked at me and said, "You know, I believe everything you have said is true. Where is your church, and when do they meet? I'd like to come and worship with you this Saturday." What an exciting response! We were so thrilled about her desire to attend church that we forgot to tell her anything about jewelry or make-up or what she ought to wear when she came. After she left the meeting, some of us stayed by to pray and thank the Lord for the miracle He was working in Maria's life. We could hardly imagine the joy of her guardian angel who had been preparing her for this moment for decades.
>
> Sabbath morning Maria showed up for church bright and early. Wanting to make a good impression, she had dressed in all her finest—fashionable suit, big hat, dangling ear rings, bright red lipstick—and sported a brand new Bible under her arm. She was greeted at the door by one of our deacons who hadn't been to the Bible study and hadn't seen the miracle. All he saw was a woman who dressed very much like people in the world. With a sigh of disgust, he looked at Maria as she approached

the greeter's desk and said, "Well . . . I can see that you're not one of our women!"

Poor Maria felt devastated. Her enthusiasm crumpled into embarrassment as she fled from our church, never to return again. She told me later that she ran from our place feeling like some sort of "tainted woman." At home, she locked herself in her room and cried for two hours. Several times we offered our deepest apologies, but Maria was unwilling to take the risk again.

Six months later, Maria called to invite me to her baptism. Our Bible study had effectively convinced her that Catholic doctrine was wrong, but she needed to find a church that accepted her. She landed in a small, friendly Baptist church. Although the Baptists didn't teach the Bible the same way we did, they provided the genuine warmth and love she needed to make the change.

Oh, how God's heart must have ached. Somehow we have created a real monster (beast?) within Adventism—members like this deacon who are more concerned with being right than with being loving. Apparently the deacon forgot the words of Christ, "They that be whole need not a physician, but they that are sick. Go ye and learn what that meaneth, 'I will have mercy and not sacrifice . . .'" (Matthew 9:12-13).

Apparently he hadn't read this startling comment from Ellen White:

> If we would humble ourselves before God, and be *kind and courteous and tenderhearted and pitiful,* there would be *one hundred* conversions to the truth where now there is only one. (*Testimonies,* vol. 9, p. 189, emphasis supplied)

Reflection

How can your church prevent what happened to Maria? What are some subtle, less obvious ways that such a thing can happen to people?

I enjoy attending weddings—the freshness, the nervous laughter, the lovey-dovey smiles. One of my favorite marriages occurred over two thousand years ago and was performed by the Author of love, Jesus Christ. Instead of marrying two people, however, He brought together two concepts, two huge truths. Those two truths are the Great Commission and the Great Commandment: "Go ye therefore" and "Thou shalt love thy neighbor" (Matthew 28:19 and 22:39). We might even add, "What God hath joined together, let no man put asunder."

Jesus taught that the way to fulfill the Great Commission is to fulfill the Great Commandment. These two commands are simply two sides of the same coin. Jesus modeled that concept for us two thousand years ago, and we are told that His method cannot be improved upon. May the following Spirit of Prophecy plea burn into our minds:

> Christ's method alone will give true success in reaching the people. The Saviour mingled with men as one who desired their good. He showed His sympathy for them, ministered to their needs, and won their confidence. Then He bade them, "Follow Me." (*Ministry of Healing,* p. 143, emphasis supplied)

Notice our Lord's sequence:

- The Saviour mingled with men
- as one who desired their good

- He showed His sympathy for them
- ministered to their needs
- won their confidence
- *Then* He bade them, "Follow Me"

Contrast that with the sequence we often employ:

- Send a brochure
- Ask them to come to where we are
- Teach them the truth
- Ask them to follow truth

Distressingly different. First, Jesus formed a relationship with people. He demonstrated His love. He got to know them and listened to them. He got close to them. And the Spirit of Prophecy says that this method *alone* will give true success. Why do we so often look for shortcuts? Evidently, we don't really trust Jesus' method, or else we would give it top priority.

We have allowed ourselves to become experts at spreading information instead of experts at love. We pay thousands of dollars to the mailman so he will go around our city or town and invite everyone to come hear our information. People are crying out for someone to listen, someone to wipe a tear, someone to cool a burning brow, and we give them a brochure, and that by proxy.

How would we feel if, instead of sending Jesus, God had sent a brochure? "God so loved the world that He sent a brochure." "By this shall all men know that you are my disciples, if you mail a lot of brochures." God's most powerful invitation is still His love seen in the lives of His followers. God's most compelling brochure is you.

It is not a question of whether we should be concerned with information *or* relationships. Both are vital. They work together. But in terms of outreach, the vast majority of people in the United States will not care how much we *know* until they know how much we *care*. What will secular people care about the 2,300-day prophecy when they don't even believe in God?

Again the Spirit of Prophecy is clear:

> The strongest argument in favor of the gospel is a loving and lovable Christian. (*Ministry of Healing,* p. 470)

> Men will believe, not what the minister preaches, but what the church lives. (*Testimonies,* vol. 9, p. 21)

Reflection

"In all honesty, the greatest challenge I face in getting close to non-Adventists is. . . ." (finish the sentence)

Before the 1950s, American society was strong on relationships but starving for information. Today, society's needs are just the opposite. People today are flooded with information and starving for relationships. People's felt needs have shifted dramatically, but our methods have not. Our tendency to make information-spreading our primary goal has led us to rely far too heavily on radio and TV to reach the public.

> As strange as it may seem to us in the 20th Century, the most rapid growth of the church occurred long before the advent of modern Media. There was no television, radio, or printed page. First century evangels had just one medium for communicating God's Good News—love. (*Who Cares About Love,* Win Arn, Carroll Nyquist, and Charles Arn, p. 114)

If people feel truly loved first, they will often accept the information very quickly later. Proclamation of information certainly has its rightful place and can reach certain people initially that no other method can. This lesson is not intended to devalue that method. It is an attempt to address the suffocating imbalance that results from relying almost exclusively on proclamation, when both the Scriptures and the felt needs of society dictate that relationships must be paramount.

A survey of recent converts to Adventism revealed that 65-70 percent of people become Seventh-day Adventists primarily through relationships with friends and relatives. The remaining percentages are scattered in much smaller amounts among programs, pastor, Sabbath school, seminars, radio/TV, and so on (Growth Leadership Seminar, NADEI). Relationships with friends and relatives hold by far the greatest potential for growth, yet few Adventists are taught how to develop close friendships with non-Adventists. It is not central to our strategy.

Paul Little portrays the problem in this passage:

> About once every six months the pressure to witness used to reach explosive heights inside me. Not knowing any better, I would suddenly lunge at someone and spout all my verses with a sort of glazed stare in my eye. I honestly didn't expect any response. As soon as my victim indicated lack of interest, I'd begin to edge away from him with a sigh of relief and the consoling thought, "All that will live godly in Christ Jesus shall suffer persecution" (2 Timothy 3:12). Duty done, I'd draw back into my martyr's shell for another six months' hibernation, until the internal pressure again became intolerable and drove me out. It really shocked me when I finally realized that I, not the cross, was offending people. My inept, unwittingly rude, even stupid approach to them was responsible for their rejection of me and the gospel message.
>
> As the Scripture says, "He who has friends must be a friend himself" (Proverbs 18:24). The art of friendship has been lost by many Christians because they feel their time is being wasted when it's not invested in a specifically religious [discussion with non-Christians]. To be a friend may involve listening to a neighbor's troubles or participating with him in non-religious activities that are of mutual interest socially. It means actively seeking opportunities to show love by running errands, baby-sitting, and performing any other mundane but practical service that will demonstrate the love of Christ. . . . If we are committing our time to the Lord, the Holy Spirit will, in His time, give natural opportunities to speak about the Saviour (*How to Give Away Your Faith,* Paul Little, p. 30, 32).

Reflection

Would you dare be seen hanging around people who are drinking a lot of beer? Would it be OK to make some of these people our best friends, for Christ's sake, just as they are? Why or why not?

The primary language of the church has to be relationships. We serve a big God and have a big message. Packaged in love, that message can be far more potent than we imagine.

> The largest Christian church in the world, with more than 700,000 members, is located in Korea. In spite of the church's enormous size, every member feels cared for because they also have 50,000 small groups. The senior pastor was once asked how much he expected the church to grow in the coming year. "We will add about 100,000 new converts next year," he replied. Stunned, the interviewer inquired how such amazing growth could be accomplished. The pastor replied, "At the

> beginning of the year we ask each of our small groups to spend that year loving just two people to Christ. You see, 2 x 50,000 equals 100,000 converts. Love is the key." I long for the day when we can trust the power of love so fully.

Event versus Process

Because Lovesharing is built on relationships, making contacts with non-Adventists becomes an ongoing process, not a spring or fall event.

> Imagine a farmer who owns five hundred acres of fertile land and employs one hundred farm hands. His large, well-kept barn contains various pieces of seldom-used farming equipment. Corn is their preferred crop, but farm workers rarely plow, weed, or plant. They hardly ever water or fertilize. In fact, very little farming at all is done during the year—until fall. It is then that the gleaming reaper is cranked up and put into service. High up in the cab the farmer steers toward the untended fields while the farm hands applaud vigorously. The farmer motors back and forth over the cropless ground. A few wind-born seeds from other farms that landed on his acreage months ago have sprouted into an occasional stalk. The large reaper scoops these up and deposits them in the bin. Back at the barn the farmer pulls eight ears of corn out of the reaper and shows them to the workers. Together they rejoice over another excellent harvest. Tragically, this farmer sees farming as an annual event rather than a year-long process.

I had hardly begun pastoring my new district when one of our local church elders told me, "This church hasn't had any baptisms for quite a while. I think we ought to get an evangelist in here and have some meetings." I asked, "How many non-Adventists do you folks currently have coming to church?" He couldn't think of any. I continued, "How many close non-Adventist friends do you think the members have?" He didn't think there were any of those either. "How many Bible studies are the members giving at present?" "Oh, I think the previous pastor had a few." No plowing, no planting, weeding, or watering. So bring in the reaper? Any farmer could have told him such a plan was unworkable. Healthy churches should have people flowing into them all year long.

Public evangelistic meetings and seminars, in their proper sphere, can be excellent tools for soul winning. Advertising can be another useful tool. But both have been severely abused and misused by churches. In farming, 95 percent of the effort should be done before the reaper is ever brought out of the barn. Even then the farmer checks to see if the harvest is ready. We have come to the place where 95 percent of the effort is invested in the reaping meetings themselves and the aftermath. Somehow it has all gotten backwards. In some ways the good has, indeed, become the enemy of the best. It is a question of balance and proportion.

"But Kim, can't evangelistic meetings serve a valuable function by attracting entirely new interests, out of the blue, through advertising?" Of course. But let's recognize that in America it is a high-risk strategy. These new interests are won by a stranger and join a church of strangers. Members often feel these new converts are "the pastor's people" and don't take personal responsibility for assimilating them into church life. Unless the new members' emotional and social needs are met soon, they often feel compelled to return to their old support system, no matter what we teach. Emotional and social needs dictate many people's long-term choices far more than objective truth. We must learn to look beyond the excitement of opening night and measure success in terms of what happens to people in the months and years that follow.

Church-Centered versus People-Centered:

Church-centered evangelism has as its main focus "building up the church" or "adding members to the church." We ask non-Adventists to inconvenience themselves and come to our church, sit in our pews, listen to our information. (Is it any wonder that we have to send out 10,000 brochures to get fifty people to attend?)

Lovesharing, on the other hand, emphasizes people-centered evangelism, where the church members initiate friendly contacts with non-Adventists. People-centered evangelism shapes ministry to people's needs and offers to all a love that has no ulterior motives, no hidden agendas. It is people-centered evangelism that most closely follows the methods of Christ.

Leighton Ford captures the spirit of people-centered ministry here:

> Not long ago I talked with a Christian woman who was trying to restructure her life in order to make contacts [with non-Christians]. She went on a tour to Greece with a non-Christian group. She said, "I have my orders. I believe it is possible to go to too many prayer meetings, though not to pray too much. At present, I don't even have permission [from the Lord] to go to the missionary circle in my church, although I believe wholeheartedly in missions. But I did get orders from the Lord to join a Great-Books Club." She reported that the discussions were not so profound, but there were no holds barred in discussing her faith with the group. (*Good News Is For Sharing,* p. 109-110)

In the parable of the sheep and the goats in Matthew 25:31-46 (please read), Jesus reveals the people-centered work He expects His church to be doing in the world in the last days. He talks about the "sheep people" who have made love the central theme of their lives. These love dispensers feed those who are hungry—hungry not just for potatoes and carrots but for love. They clothe those who feel naked—physically, emotionally, spiritually. They quench people's thirst for acceptance and a listening ear. The Holy Spirit fills these sheep people with intense concern for their families, the people at work, the people sitting next to them at church, the neighbors across the street, the attendants at the gas station.

On the other hand, Jesus' parable also talks about "goat people." Right here is a very important point from the parable that we can easily miss—goat love is selective. These people say they would have been more than willing to help if they had only known it was Christ they were ministering to. Jesus' point here is that it shouldn't matter at all who they are loving. Nothing else should matter except that someone is in need.

Isn't it true in our outreach that the people who respond to our efforts and want Bible studies get that 95 percent of our continued attention? In a typical church "interest file," those who do not want Bible studies are gradually pushed toward the back and eventually forgotten. Suppose we find out later that one of the names that got pushed to the back of the interest file really does want Bible studies after all? Can't you hear some of us saying something to them like the following:

"Oh, I'm sorry. If I'd only known you were a spiritually interested person I would have spent more time with you."

"Oh, if I had only known you wanted baptism, I would have paid more attention to you."

And doesn't that also sound remarkably like the goat people in the parable: "Oh, if we'd only known it was You, Jesus!" "Oh, if we'd only known you were worth our time and effort!" The crucial point here is that any time we love people *in order that* they will do something or believe something, then we are acting like goat people. Anytime we love people while secretly hoping that our love will get them to accept Christ or become an Adventist, we are goats. Goat love has ulterior motives. It uses love to manipulate people to change.

Reflection

When I think about loving others unconditionally, I feel that. . . . (choose one and tell why)

a. It seems impossible most of the time
b. I really have a hard time picturing what that would be like
c. I need to be loved like that myself first
d. I'm afraid that others will take advantage of such love
e. Other:

True love is like the sun. It shines simply because it is the sun and can't help shining. Of course, all kinds of good things result—like vegetation and life. But these are not the reason for the sunshine, only its effects. Even if nothing grew, the sun would shine in full intensity still. Attempts to use love as a tool corrupt love and will be perceived as such.

"But Kim," you might say, "shouldn't I try to get people to accept Christ?" Of course, if they are ready. The point is that getting them to accept Christ is not your motive or reason for loving them. Ironically, the very thing that will enable people to accept Christ the fastest is for them to perceive that you'll love them just as much even if they don't. Simply loving others for love's sake alone can have enormous fallout in the form of changed lives and spiritual interest. And when that occurs, of course we will be glad to point people to God. But even if that response never comes, our love will not be diminished or withdrawn. "Love spoken can be turned aside. Love demonstrated is irresistible" (Stanley Mooneyham as quoted in *Who Cares About Love,* p. 104).

Individual Approach versus Team Approach:
Because our primary focus has often been on reaping, we tend to see only a tiny portion of the process of conversion—the end. We easily forget that God has used many Christians over many years to bring a person to the point where he or she is interested in spiritual things. If we focus primarily on reaping, we are in danger of viewing the individual efforts of the reaper as the key to success. In reality, God depended on a team and every team member's part was equally important. In this approach, every team member gets a "star in her crown," no matter what part in the process she played. (Why do we use this "star" motivation anyway?)

Imagine non-Christians as being like a water pitcher. The love we show them becomes the individual drops of water that go into the pitcher. In this analogy, as the water level increases, so does the person's spiritual interest. Perhaps they don't sense any personal need for God until the pitcher is 90 percent full. At the time, we don't know which drop we are in the filling process. We may be the first drop, or we may be the last one that makes it spill over into Bible studies. Which drop do you think is most important? Obviously, all are equally valuable. It takes all the little droplets of love to work, over time, as a team.

We could also use what I call the Spiritual Interest Line, graphed following:

Spiritual Interest Line

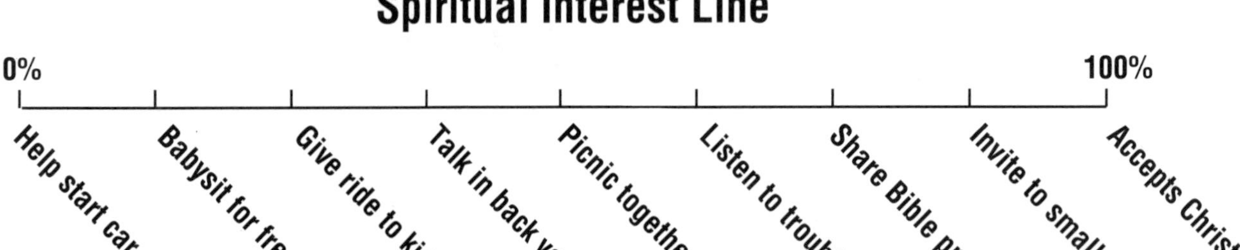

At zero, people have no spiritual interest at all. At perhaps 90 percent they become aware of a need for God in their life. At 100 percent they accept Christ. People around us are at all stages along their own Spiritual Interest Line. It is God's Spirit that moves them along that line from left to right. The tool He uses is our love. The Spiritual Interest Line is made up of many different individual links until it becomes a long chain. Over time, as various Christians meet the felt needs of a person, the Spirit takes those acts of love and forges new links. The concept of lovesharing is to cooperate with the Spirit in discovering where people are along that line and meeting whatever needs are appropriate to that time in the spiritual journey. It would be inappropriate to minister to people who are at 5 percent as if they were at 95 percent. The opposite is also true. Our job is to be sensitive to the Spirit's working and discover what ministry the next link should be, from running errands to sharing about Christ. It usually takes many different people over time for the Spirit to form the full chain of circumstances that leads to conversion.

Note one author's description of this process:

> [Lovesharing] is taking the initiative to bring a person one step closer to Christ. . . . That definition lifts the load of guilt from people. They see that they do not have to be the entire process, but just a part, which may be initiating a friendship, cultivating a relationship, encouraging someone to consider Christ, or being the reaper who sees the person accept the Saviour.
>
> It seems that people usually think of successful evangelism as leading someone to Christ. A lot of frustration and inactivity can result with this understanding. . . . Success in evangelism [is] taking the initiative in the power of the Holy Spirit to help the person move one step closer in the process of coming to Christ. [Christians] are . . . to identify where their friend is in their spiritual journey. Then they determine what initiative should be taken in helping their friend move one step closer to the point of conversion. When believers understand that, evangelism becomes manageable and possible. (*Church Disciple Newsletter,* May, 1992)

Working Around Members versus Working Through Them:
This may come as a surprise, but God asks us to minister to non-Adventists not primarily for their benefit but for ours. Ministering to non-Adventists is one of God's primary tools to make us like Himself.

> God could have reached His object in saving sinners without our aid; but in order for us to develop a character like Christ's, we must share in His work. (*The Desire of Ages,* p. 142)

A church whose outreach strategy takes an end-run around the membership by depending on a few experts tragically short-circuits God's plan. Churches must choose ministries that work *through* the members rather than *around* them, or else they deprive members of the opportunity to become like Christ.

Review Questions

1. Someone has commented, "We cannot create spiritual interest in anyone, we can only discover what the Holy Spirit is already doing." How could such a concept help alleviate guilt?

2. What is the greatest challenge the concept of lovesharing poses for you? How do you feel this Bible study group can help you meet that challenge?

3. You are the manager of a department store. The staff gets along very well. All your employees know you are a Seventh-day Adventist, and you have tried to live Christ's love. But in the past seven years, not one of them has shown any definite spiritual interest. What do you do?

Love in Action

My Choice:

Go to a shopping mall near your home this week. Sit down and observe the customers for a half an hour. As you watch them pass by, ask yourself how your church could reach out to them more effectively with the love of Christ.

Your Choice:

Learning to be a Group: Each member of the group is as responsible for how a particular meeting goes as is the group leader. It is a shared responsibility. Don't be a spectator. Invest in the success of your group.

Love in Action Feedback: Did you see some interesting people at the mall? (Hope you left the charge card home!) What did you feel as you watched these folks pass by?

Ice Breaker: Who was one of the most interesting or inspiring people you ever met? Why?

Disciple Makers

NASA engineers at Mission Control in Houston stared intently at the data parading across their consoles as the ill-fated, unmanned launch proceeded. "Three, two, one, blast off! We have blast off." The multimillion-dollar rocket easily cleared pad 2, and everyone could feel the nervousness slacken slightly. Twenty miles down range now and no glitches. One scientist muttered excitedly, "Go, baby go!" as he watched the receding image dance on a nearby television tracking screen. The engineer at the main console was the first to notice an almost imperceptible deviation in the flight path. His tense, monotone voice reported, "We have an anomaly." The rocket then pitched down sharply and within seconds plunged into the rolling Atlantic. What had gone wrong? After several days of investigation, experts fingered the onboard computer program as the culprit. Deep within millions of lines of computer code, they found one wrong word. One word sent an impeccably crafted rocket off course and destroyed years of planning and painstaking effort. A tiny mistake with huge consequences.

In similar fashion, a serious problem in another kind of code has been sending many churches throughout North America off course for decades. As church-growth experts observed churches throughout the United States in recent years, they saw spiritual weakness and anemic growth statistics and asked why. Their search for answers led them to examine the biblical "program" that everyone was using for guidance and direction. After careful study they discovered an important glitch. The translators of the King James Version had used a wrong word in the Great Commission of Matthew 28:19-20. In that version, Jesus is quoted as saying, "Go ye therefore, and *teach* all nations. . . ."

It is the word "teach" that is the problem. The original Greek comes from the word "manthano," which does not mean "teach" at all. The Greek word for "teach" is a different word entirely. "Manthano" means "to make disciples." What Jesus is really saying in the Great Commission is, "Go ye therefore and *make disciples* of all nations. . . ."

"But Kim," someone might say, "I don't like Greek anyway, and it seems as if you're making a mountain out of a molehill here." Hardly. The word teach has the connotation of "lecture" and "sharing of information." We get mental images of classrooms and teachers and pupils with pencils and notebooks. The phrase "make disciples," however, conjures up entirely different images. It includes teaching, to be sure, but much more. When the followers of Christ heard Him give His mandate in Matthew 28 to make disciples, they undoubtedly thought of what Christ had done for them personally over the previous three years. Ask James, John, Peter, and Matthew, men whose lives were completely transformed, what "make disciples" meant, and they would undoubtedly define that phrase by their own experience. To them disciple making had to do with the whole person, not only the mind. It affected the attitude, character, loyalties, and whole outlook on life. Disciple making focused on building people in depth. It dealt with not only what they knew but who they were. Disciple making led people into a deep relationship with God and guided them into meaningful ministry based on their spiritual gifts.

For us today the following definition of disciple making seems close to the mark:

Discipling others is the process by which Christians, with a life worth emulating, commit themselves for an extended period of time to a few individuals in order to—

1. Help them find assurance of salvation in Christ
2. Develop their hearts and minds to Spirit-filled maturity
3. Equip them for ministry and the discipling of others

So what difference has all this made in the church? Because the church viewed the Great Commission primarily as teaching, we felt that we were finished once people were instructed in the doctrines of the church. Instead of discipling people, we simply taught them Bible facts. We got into the familiar "Dip'em and Drop'em" syndrome. We saw witnessing as mainly sharing information. So we wound up with many members who knew a lot about doctrine but did not have maturity of character or a vital connection with God. They didn't develop a meaningful ministry or plumb the depths of such concepts as lordship, duty, and love. Most new members were baptized but not discipled. We wound up with Laodicea.

Reflection

Share how someone outside of your immediate family gave you significant help in your own Christian experience.Would you call this a form of discipling?

Christ's Great Commission has one overall goal—making disciples**.** He lists three means for achieving that goal—go, baptize, teach.

> Therefore go and make disciples of all nations, baptizing them in the name of the Father and of the Son and of the Holy Spirit and teaching them to obey everything I have commanded you." (Matthew 28:19)

Notice how one Adventist leader analyzed these elements of the Great Commission:

> Neither going, baptizing, nor teaching are ends in themselves; they are all means to the end of discipling. . . . We hear a great deal about baptizing. We talk about teaching true Bible doctrines. Neither of these activities is an ultimate end of the gospel commission. They are merely means to the end of discipling. . . . Jesus said the church's business is making disciples. To make disciples, we need to go, we need to baptize, we need to teach. But these are not our primary business. If these become ends in themselves, if we ever concentrate on any of them rather than on making disciples, we'll soon be out of business." (Floyd Bresee, *Ministry,* April 1990)

Jesus made teaching a part of the process of discipling, to be sure. But even here, we need to re-examine His plan. Notice carefully what Jesus told us to teach: "Teach them to obey all things whatsoever I have commanded you. . . ."

"Whatsoever I commanded you" takes in a lot of territory. Christ is talking here about far more than simply making sure that church members understand Adventist doctrine, as important as that is. It encompasses all the insights and perspectives Jesus shared in the Gospels. Such teaching impacts every area of a person's life.

Notice also *how* Jesus taught His disciples. It was accomplished mostly by example and association. His truths were mostly "caught," not "taught." As one author writes,

> [The] religious teachers of His day insisted upon their disciples adhering strictly to certain rituals and formulas of knowledge, whereby they were distinguished from others; whereas Jesus asked only that His disciples follow Him. Knowledge was not communicated by the Master in terms of laws and dogmas, but in the living personality of One who walked among them. . . . Knowledge was gained by association before it was understood by explanation. (*The Master Plan of Evangelism,* Robert Coleman, p. 38-39)

The Spirit of Prophecy underscores Jesus' unique disciple making methods:

> These men [the twelve] He purposed to train and educate as the leaders of His church. They in turn were to educate others. . . . By personal contact and association, Christ trained them for His service. . . . In all His work, He was training them for individual labor, to be extended as their numbers increased, and eventually to reach to the uttermost parts of the earth. (*Acts of the Apostles,* p. 17, 32)

This mentoring strategy of patiently growing people through personal association and accountability has become a lost art. God's plan of having one person pour his life into another has been reduced to periodic weekend training seminars. Christ had success because He took time to truly build people in depth. Because personal association is such an important part of disciple making, the process cannot be rushed and cannot be done primarily out of a manual.

Today we are not at all used to doing what the Great Commission requires. We are far better spiritual obstetricians than we are pediatricians.

> The crisis at the heart of the church is that we give disciple-making lip service, but do not practice it. . . . Churches are too little like training centers to shape up the saints and too much like cardiopulmonary wards at the local hospital. . . . We are too easily satisfied with conventional success: bodies, bucks and buildings." (*The Disciple Making Pastor,* Bill Hull, p. 12, 15)

I am so very thankful that the command to make disciples is surrounded by references to the Godhead:

> All power is given to Me in heaven and in earth. (verse 18)
>
> . . . in the name of the Father, and of the Son and of the Holy Spirit. (verse 19)
>
> . . . I am with you alway, even to the end of the world. (verse 20)

Jesus emphasizes here that successful disciple making depends on the Godhead working in and through the entire process. All growth occurs through His strength.

Reflection

If you were one of Jesus' original disciples, what specific insight into successful living would He most likely share as you walked together along the dusty roads of Judea?

When Jesus chose the discipling strategy to reach the world, there were, I'm sure, many who thought He had made a huge mistake. During Christ's three-and-one-half years of ministry, He seems to have spent an inordinate amount of time with just twelve people. He did not ignore the multitudes, but it is obvious that the twelve were His primary concern, and even within that group He focused extra time on just three—Peter, James, and John. Shouldn't He have tried to get His message out to as many as possible as fast as possible? Shouldn't He have spent every available minute preaching to the masses? Why did He give so much attention to so few when His time was so limited?

The reason is that Jesus worked on the principle of multiplication instead of addition. He could have spent all His time adding thousands to His list of followers during His brief public ministry, but they could not have been ministered to in depth. They would have captured only a fleeting glimpse of His character and life. He was not simply trying to teach a course on what to know, He was teaching a course on how to live. These thousands would not have had the experience or maturity necessary to multiply themselves by discipling others. After He returned to heaven, the growth of the church would have slowed dramatically and His new movement probably would have floundered completely.

Instead, Jesus chose to work with a few and bring them to the point where they could effectively disciple others. These new disciples would then multiply themselves by doing the same for others, and those in turn would disciple still others.

Jesus knew that multiplication is a powerful strategy. Note the following example:

> Some time ago there was a display at the Museum of Science and Industry in Chicago. It featured a checkerboard with 1 grain of wheat on the first square, 2 on the second, 4 on the third, then 8, 16, 32, 64, 128, etc. Somewhere down the board, there were so many grains of wheat on the square that some were spilling over into neighboring squares—so here the demonstration stopped. Above the checkerboard display was a question: "At this rate of doubling every square, how much grain would you have on the checkerboard by the time you reached the 64th square?" To find the answer to this riddle, you punched a button on the console in front of you, and the answer flashed on a little screen above the board. "Enough to cover the entire subcontinent of India 50 feet deep." (*Disciples Are Made Not Born,* Walter A. Henrichsen, p. 137-138)

Notice what could happen if we applied Jesus' multiplication strategy to modern evangelism:

> Suppose a Pastor Ted won 1,000 people every day. At the end of the first year, there would be 365,000 new believers. That is the principle of addition—1,000 added every day.
>
> Suppose another person in one year led one person to Christ and spent that year building, teaching, and training that individual to grow to maturity and to give witness of his faith and build up others. At the end of the first year, those engaged in a discipling ministry would number two.
>
> During the second year, Pastor Ted continues to lead 1,000 to Christ each day, making his total 730,000 people after two years. During that second year, the two people engaged in a discipling ministry go out and lead not 1,000 per day to Christ, but only one person each for the entire year. Time is spent with those individuals until, at the end of

the year, they are able to spiritually reproduce themselves. Therefore, at the end of the second year, the disciples now total four. If this process were to continue indefinitely, with Pastor Ted "adding" and the discipler "multiplying" each year, the total numbers of converts when compared at later dates would reveal the following:

Year	Evangelist	Discipler
1	365,000	2
2	730,000	4
10	3,650,000	1,024
19	6,935,000	524,288
20	7,300,000	1,048,576
25	9,125,000	33,554,432
26	9,490,000	67,108,864
27	9,855,000	134,217,728
184	67,160,000	

It is very easy to see that initially, the process of multiplication in discipling others is slower than the process of addition. However, when the discipler reaches year 26, he has had a part in the winning of a total number of people that the evangelist will not reach for another 158 years. In other words, the number reached by the discipler by year 26 is not reached by the evangelist until year 184. In addition to all this, we do not have just converts in the discipling column, but rather individuals who are built up in Christ and able to reproduce themselves spiritually. Also, the discipler would reach the world's population in 32 years. The evangelist would reach the world 10,960 years from now. (*Successful Discipling,* Allen Hadidian, p. 44-45)

It is this kind of multiplication strategy to which Jesus pointed when He said in the Great Commission, "Go ye therefore and make disciples." Anything less is a distortion of His plan. One author puts his finger on the challenge facing the church today when he writes:

> The church has tried to get world evangelization without disciple making. The impetuousness of human nature and cultural pressure to get quick results have caused [churches] to take every shortcut. Shortcuts don't work and most of the time we end up starting over again. Only one road leads to world evangelism: disciple making. (*The Disciple Making Pastor,* Bill Hull, p. 23)

REFLECTION

As you look at your local church's growth over the past ten to fifteen years, what are the baptisms, on average, each year? Is that evidence of addition or multiplication?

For Jesus to commit so fully to a multiplication strategy took enormous insight and courage, and it will take no less on our part today. It is, in fact, just such a strategy that most effectively addresses the most fundamental purpose for the Adventist Church's existence. The Great Controversy theme dictates that we not only reach out to the lost, but that we do so in such as way that we build people to the glory of God. Discipling is not just a nifty way to reach more people quicker, it is a plan that makes the revelation of God's love through the lives of His followers central to its purpose.

Besides what Jesus said in the Great Commission about His overall disciple making strategy, He also spoke elsewhere about specific goals and purposes He had in mind as He discipled people. These specifics can help us to focus our own disciple making efforts today.

Purposes Of Disciple Making:

1. **First, Jesus talked about self-denial and cross bearing**.

> And whosoever doth not bear his cross, and come after me, cannot be my disciple. (Luke 14:27)

The apostle Paul expanded this theme when he wrote in Galatians 2:20,

> I am crucified with Christ, nevertheless I live; yet not I, but Christ lives in me. And the life which I now live in the flesh I live by the faith of the Son of God.

Each day Paul had to reckon his old self to be dead and buried. All his old ambitions, prejudices, and self-centered attitudes were crucified. "Nonetheless," Paul exclaimed, "I am alive, but it is an entirely new me! It is Christ who has taken up residence inside this old body!" A disciple is first of all willing to climb up on the cross of Christ and let selfishness and independence die daily.

2. **Christ went on to describe a true disciple's relationship to His words.**

> Then said Jesus. . . . If ye continue in my word, then are ye my disciples indeed. (John 8:31)

To be "in" Jesus' word implies far more than being a casual reader or observer. This is no periodic contact. His instruction here is similar to what He said in John 15:5: "I am the Vine, ye are the branches. He that abideth in me and I in him, the same bringeth forth much fruit, for without Me ye can do nothing."

Continuing in Christ's words and abiding in Him are two sides of the same coin.

3. **Jesus also talked about lordship and commitment**.

> The disciple is not above his master, nor the servant above his lord. (Matthew 10:24)

One author gives the following definition of lordship:

> Grace is God's willingness to commit Himself totally to us. Lordship is our willingness to commit ourselves totally to God. (*Disciples Are Made Not Born,* p. 26)

The story is told of a young man named Kenos who lived on a South Sea island many years ago. One day foreigners came in ships and subjugated the island people, turning them into slaves. A heavyset man with gruff manners and large beard took over Kenos' hut, forcing him at gun point to be his servant. The man asked, "Kenos, will you serve me?" But Kenos did not say a single word. He simply carried out his taskmaster's commands. Every day came the same question, "Kenos, will you serve me?" followed by the same unbroken silence. Over and over this one-sided exchange repeated itself as months turned into dreary years.

> Finally, the harsh, oppressive stranger died of old age. Kenos dragged the man's limp body in a blanket out to a high cliff and shoved the corpse over the edge in disgust. Kenos then straightened, looked out over the open ocean and shouted at the top of his lungs, "No!"

Thankfully, our Lord Jesus Christ is not interested in such forced service from fear. He does not value obedience that is rooted in a desire to avoid punishment. He knows that an outward Yes can mask a defiant, inner No. Therefore He asks for the allegiance of love. He asks for our voluntary submission, as disciples, to His infinite wisdom and sacrificial care.

4. The greatest characteristic of a disciple is found in John 13:35—love.

> By this shall all men know that ye are my disciples, if ye have love one to another.

Overall, disciples need to be growing and maturing in four critical areas:

1. Knowledge (of God's will and Word)
2. Character and attitude
3. Sense of belonging (to God and fellow church members)
4. Ministry skill

The goal is to bring these four areas into balance in people's lives.

Reflection

> Of the four critical areas mentioned above, which one are you currently struggling with the most? What would help?

As Adventist churches today attempt to implement a disciple making strategy, they are faced with an increasing crisis of availability among their members. The problem has been gathering steam for years. For various reasons, different generations in our pews are hesitating to make significant time commitments to the local church.

The older generation that is near or over retirement age grew up during a time when institutions were generally seen as helpful and trustworthy. The federal government, for example, could be trusted because they brought the country successfully through World War II. This confidence in institutions led to product loyalty as well. "I always buy Chevrolets," was a typical comment. In the past the church benefitted from such institutional loyalty because it could count on this generation of church members to be present each Sabbath regardless of how boring Sabbath school might be or how ineffective the sermons were. They gave the church a steady base of workers that would be involved, no matter what. On the other hand, the church often took this loyalty for granted and failed to examine its programs and services to make sure they were meeting people's real needs. Many members of this older generation are now at a time in their lives when they feel they have done their fair share and want to see the younger ones pick up the ball and run with it.

By contrast the baby boomer generation, born between 1946 and 1964, has little institutional loyalty. They grew up at a time when the federal government was riddled with corruption and widely ridiculed for its failed policies. They have little product loyalty either. They don't particularly care whether a car comes from Chevrolet or Toyota. They are committed to quality and effectiveness. As a result, churches that cling to outmoded programs and services without assessing them for usefulness are leaving hoards of boomers on the sidelines, tuned out, bored, and disenchanted.

Finally, the 20 to 30 age group faces the pressure of finishing educational degrees and establishing careers. Add to this the fact that this group is highly mobile, and we have a set of factors that often derail their desire to get meaningfully involved in church life.

In addition, most age groups need to have both spouses work, which further detracts from their ability or willingness to make long-term commitments to ministry.

These facts and trends add up to a huge challenge for the Adventist church of the 1990s and beyond. The older generation needs to know they are vitally needed still and that there can be no retirement from spiritual growth. The baby boomers need to help shape church life so that it is more vibrant and needs-oriented. The younger members need to have access to flexible, short-term ministry opportunities. We also need to pay more attention to helping people minister through their every day lives and not simply in traditional church programs. Any church that wants to take disciple making seriously will recognize these generational differences and make whatever adjustments are necessary to develop a broad-based sense of involvement among its members.

Today we hear much talk about the great outpouring of the Holy Spirit and the Second Coming of Christ. Although we all hope that these events will take place soon, we must remember that they are dependent on certain events taking place within the church first. Even though she doesn't use the phrase disciple making, Ellen White points to that concept as one of the most critical factors influencing the end of time:

> The great outpouring of the Spirit of God, which lightens the whole earth with His glory, will not come until we have an enlightened people, that know by experience what it means to be laborers together with God. When we have entire, wholehearted consecration to the service of Christ, God will recognize the fact by an outpouring of His Spirit without measure; but this will not be while the largest portion of the church are not laborers together with God. (*Christian Service,* p. 253)

The Adventist church today needs to take seriously the full implications of the Great Commission and Jesus' central focus on disciple making. Robert Coleman states the challenge:

> Merely because we are busy, or even skilled, doing something does not necessarily mean that we are getting anything accomplished. The question must always be asked: Is it worth doing? And does it get the job done? This is a question that should be posed continually in relation to the evangelistic activity of the church. Are our efforts to keep things going fulfilling the great commission of Christ? Do we see an ever-expanding company of dedicated men reaching the world with the Gospel as a result of our ministry? That we are busy in the church trying to work one program of evangelism after another cannot be denied. But are we accomplishing our objective? (*The Master Plan of Evangelism,* p. 11-12)

Review Questions

1. What kind of person(s) would you choose to disciple you at present? Why?

2. If a young Christian asked you to disciple/mentor them for one year, what would your emphasis be? What strengths would you bring to that responsibility?

3. How do we balance a sense of urgency about the Second Coming of Christ with the slow, long-term effort that disciple making requires?

Love in Action

My Choice:

Be open enough to God's grace this week to respond to some hurt, slight, frustration, or put-down this week with unconditional love.

Your Choice:

Learning to be a Group: Come to the group in the spirit of a learner as well as a contributor. Be open to what the Holy Spirit may want to teach you. Avoid being the "answer man."

Love in Action Feedback: Were you able to respond in new ways with unconditional love to some hurt or frustration this last week?

Group Activity: Nine Dots.

Just Imagine!

My high school teacher's disheveled hair matched his rumpled clothes, quirky smile, and slightly vacant gaze. One class period he announced, "Now, students, I will come around and look right into your eyes and tell you something about yourself. OK?" Hey, why not. Staring into my glasses, he cocked his head this way and that like a robin trying to locate worms. Suddenly he straightened, then concluded, "You, my boy, like to see the big picture, the big view of things." And you know what? He was right.

For years I have searched for the big picture in Adventism. What is our church's central purpose? What is God's grand design for His remnant people? What I see of the answer has gripped my imagination and dramatically altered my spiritual focus. In this lesson we will look at some key elements of that picture.

Since the beginning of sin, God has been trying, through every means possible, to draw sinners to Himself that He might make them whole. His heart is so full of love, and He has such infinite resources, that even the most hardened sinner, the most hopeless problems, the most intractable needs, can find their answer in Him. Thousands of years ago, in Old Testament times, God chose a mind-boggling strategy to attract wayward sinners. It is a plan designed to make the Gospel practically irresistible. He decided to create church.

At age seven I made my final, irrevocable decision to leave home when mom told me I could not watch a science fiction show on TV that night at eleven. After making my fateful announcement, I stomped upstairs to pack. Mom said nothing but immediately began baking chocolate chip cookies. She knew I had to pass through the kitchen on my way to nowhere, and the cookies got me. What an irresistible smell. I took three steps out the door, did a 180 degree turn, and patched things up over sweets.

God works in a similar way. By far, God's greatest means of attracting sinners is through a revelation of His love. Many centuries ago He decided that in order to make His love as real and captivating as possible, He would build a community of believers on whom He could shower His grace. What would make this church particularly effective is not that it was made up of individual super saints. What gave it unique power is the way His followers would function together. In God's equation, one plus one equals at least three. He knows His followers can be more when joined together than when alone. It is the power of community, the power of being the body of Christ. Out of that healing fellowship flow such caring and kindness that nonbelievers on their way to nowhere can catch the fragrance of His love and come home.

The genius of church is what scientists call "synergy." Webster's defines "synergy" as "combined action greater in total effect than the sum" of the individual parts (*Webster's New World Dictionary*, Warner Books, 1979, p. 607). For instance, when all of my body parts function together in just the right way, you suddenly have much more than just a heart plus kidneys plus stomach plus muscles plus ears. You get something entirely new, something unique.You have a person. That is far greater than simply adding up what each of those body parts could do individually. You get a walking, talking, thinking human being who can speak words of encouragement and offer a helping hand to those in need.

Likewise, suppose a man is dying of thirst in a desert. An ambulance crew drives up and gives him pure oxygen. He's still thirsty. Next, they give him hydrogen gas. Thirsty still. Finally, they combine in a bottle two parts hydrogen with one part oxygen—H_2O—and presto, water. No more thirst. Oxygen and hydrogen together make something entirely new that is greater than the sum of what each could do alone. You can also put certain chemicals together, as fireflies do, and get light. And that is the fundamental key to being church. God knows that "church," when done biblically, can produce a type of love and caring that is far greater than simply adding up what each Christian could provide individually.

> When I was much too young to be dealing in real estate, I read an amazing ad on the back of a Wheaties cereal box: "For only 25 cents you too can own a piece of Alaska! Send in today along with three Wheaties box tops." What an opportunity! Visions of the Yukon and gold rush danced through my head. The box tops were no problem (I lived on Wheaties), but the 25 cents took a while. I wrapped the box tops with a rubber band, taped the money to a small piece of cardboard, stuffed it all in an envelope, and shipped it off with great expectations. Three weeks later a small package arrived with my name on it. I pulled out an impressive deed with a fancy border. It read, "This is to certify that Mr. Kim Allan Johnson owns one square inch of Alaska." I reached inside the package again and pulled out a bag of dirt. They had sent all my land in a baggie! Perhaps I missed some fine print somewhere, but it sure felt like false advertising to me.

God understands that people are skeptical of mere talk. He knows how wary they are of spiritual false advertising. That is why His plan revolves around people getting to know Him through living proof of His love. This is God's great experiment. Down through the centuries, through extraordinary sacrifice, He has attempted to build a community of believers that draws others like a magnet to the wonderful God revealed by their love.

The Scriptures talk about heaven's plan in terms of God's "glory," which is His character of love (Exodus 33:18, 19). First, God's love was to be seen in His followers. "And the glory of the Lord shall be revealed, and all flesh shall see it together" (Isaiah 40:5). Second, as God was revealed through His church, nonbelievers would come to know and accept Him as the Source. "Thou art my servant . . . in whom I will be glorified" (Isaiah 49:3).

Jesus captured these two concepts when He taught, "By this is my Father glorified, that you bear much fruit. . ." (John 15:8). God is glorified in the sense that people will be attracted to Him when they see what a difference His love makes. The glory that comes to Him is not the result of an ego trip on the part of the Godhead. They are not trying to drum up pats on the back. The praise that returns to Them is a by-product of Their loving investment in others.

Old Testament Israel

Without a doubt, God's most breathtaking attempt to implement His vision of a loving spiritual community was with the Jewish slaves in Egypt. God promised to make Abraham's seed a great nation that no man could number. Years later, however, Abraham's descendants fell into Egyptian slavery, and the promise seemed impossible to fulfill. The Israelite people became slaves for generations. They had no education, no refinement, and no higher aspiration than to survive another dreadful, meaningless day. Their sensibilities were brutalized. They knew only the motivation of Pharaoh's whip, immersed as they were for countless decades in a dark world of abuse and suffocating oppression. No one could possibly imagine the slaves as a holy nation. The onlooking universe was stunned as God chose to work with them in spite of it all.

After the Israelites left Egypt, God began revealing His purposes bit by bit. From making a golden calf to murmuring against Moses, Israel balked and backslid in the wilderness for years. Through it all, God continued to unfold His incredible vision like the petals on a rose. He planned to elevate Israel to unparalleled levels of love, fulfillment, excellence, and joy.

In order for Israel to mature in love, God provided enormous resources. He gave them helpful insights in many areas of life. He longed to help them find the most direct route possible out of self-destructive living and into spiritual, emotional, physical, and intellectual health. He planned to develop an Old Testament Church whose members shared such

- mutual support
- genuine fellowship
- maturity of outlook
- breadth of understanding
- largeness of heart and
- depth of caring
- that surrounding nations would marvel.

Orchids are one of the most gorgeous flowers in nature, but they require a warm, tropical environment in order to grow. The right surroundings can produce breathtaking flowers. In similar fashion, out of the greenhouse of Israel's wonderfully blessed, nurturing community, God planned to produce astonishing results in the lives of the Israelites and their offspring. Many would become intellectual giants (*Patriarchs and Prophets,* p. 378). Others, skilled in agriculture, would gradually restore the earth to its Edenic beauty and fertility (Isaiah 51:3). Jewish craftsmen would render products "made in Israel" superior to all others (Exodus 31:2-6). The Israelite nation would enjoy an unheard of degree of emotional and physical well-being (Deuteronomy 7:13, 15). Most of all, they would exemplify a life of love and service to others.

These results were to open pagan hearts to the amazing God who gave Himself so fully and cared so deeply. By accomplishing such a vision through slaves, at the bottom rung of humanity, it would be abundantly clear that the success must have come from God. That is why He prefaced the Ten Commandments with the preamble that is often overlooked today: "I am the Lord thy God, which have brought thee out of the land of Egypt, out of the house of bondage" (Exodus 20:2).

In this introduction God is, in effect, saying to Israel, "I want to build you into a team of winners and champions of love, committed to excellence. But don't think for a second that you can get there on your own. You will be just as dependent on Me to free you from the bondage of sin and selfishness as you were to be freed from bondage in Egypt. How many plagues were you able to produce? How many frogs were you able to summon? How many rivers did you turn to blood? How often have you parted the Red Sea? Now I will be the source of another miracle—within you."

Reflection

What kind of human environment enables you to grow best? What makes you shrivel up?

God loves all nations equally. He chose Israel as a vehicle by which every people group on earth could eventually experience His blessings. The love within Israel was supposed to spill over and spread worldwide. They were chosen to minister to others.

In a vision Isaiah saw the dramatic impact God's Israelite church would have on the surrounding heathen nations:

> Arise, shine; for thy light is come, and the glory of the Lord is risen upon thee [Israel]. . . . His glory shall be seen upon thee. And the Gentiles shall come to thy light and kings to the brightness of thy rising. (Isaiah 60:1-3)

Ambassadors from heathen nations would put their chariots in overdrive to visit Israel and learn about the God who gifted them with such preeminence (Isaiah 55:5; *Seventh-day Adventist Bible Commentary,* vol. 4, p. 29). These foreign converts would then carry the good news back to their own countries, infecting every aspect of heathen society with new life.

Although God warned Israel not to adopt heathen practices, they were never supposed to isolate themselves from their pagan neighbors (*Prophets and Kings*, p. 708). God never intended that the Israelites form an exclusive spiritual club. When the Jews chose to build spiritual walls rather than bridges, God took matters into His own hands and scattered them abroad through adversity. The ten northern tribes were dispersed as witnesses among the heathen (*Prophets and Kings*, p. 292). Joseph and other faithful Jews were given important positions in pagan Egypt, where they lived out the principles of God's Kingdom (*The Youth's Instructor*, April 8, 1897). Later, the Israelites were taken captive to Babylon, where they shared the truth about the God who saves (*The Desire of Ages* p. 28).

Nation after nation was eventually supposed to become part of Israel, until Israel's borders encompassed the whole world (Isaiah 27:6; 45:14; 14:1; *Christ's Object Lessons*, p. 288, 290). God intended that Israel become the greatest nation on earth, the "queen of kingdoms" (*The Desire of Ages*, p. 577). Our loving God wanted the "earth to be filled with joy and peace" (*Christ's Object Lessons*, p. 290). The geographic center for this vast spiritual community, the House of God in Jerusalem, would eventually "be called an house of prayer for all people" (Isaiah 56:7). Millions would glorify God from every land on earth. Sadly, however, Israel continued to splash around in spiritual mud puddles instead of wading out into God's ocean of opportunity. They chose the gutter rather than glory.

Even during Jesus' ministry on earth, Israel could have yet fulfilled God's plan of enlightening the nations.

> If the leaders and teachers at Jerusalem had received the truth Christ brought, what a missionary center their city would have been! Backslidden Israel would have been converted. A vast army would have been gathered for the Lord. And how rapidly they could have carried the gospel to all parts of the world. (*Christ's Object Lessons,* p. 232)

Tragically, despite centuries of incredibly patient effort by the Trinity, Israel ultimately spit in God's face and irrevocably said "No!" When God sent His own Son to live among them and give them as many hugs and miracles as they could tolerate, they beat Him to a pulp and nailed Him to a tree. And knowing full well the enormous privileges and destiny that Israel had squandered, God still spoke through His Son on the cross and said, "I'm so sorry it worked out this way. I'm still willing to forgive."

So Plan A went up in smoke. Have you ever poured your heart and soul into a project, only to have it blow up in your face in the end? If so, you know something of the heartbreak within the Trinity. How God felt about what "could have been" is movingly captured here in Hosea:

> Ephraim, how could I part with you? Israel, how could I give you up? My heart recoils from it, my whole being trembles at the thought. (Hosea 11:8)

The Desire of Ages describes the scene as Jesus later weeps over the stubborn, rebellious city of Jerusalem:

> They are surprised and disappointed to see His [Jesus'] eyes fill with tears, and His body rock to and fro like a tree before the tempest, while a wail of anguish bursts from his quivering lips. What a sight was this for angels to behold! Their loved Commander in an agony of tears! (*The Desire of Ages,* p. 575)

What went so terribly wrong? For one, Israel lost sight of her high privileges (*Acts of the Apostles*, p. 14). Helen Keller was once asked, "What would be worse than being born blind?" She replied, "To have sight without vision." That's exactly what happened to Old Testament Israel. They forgot their destiny (John Maxwell, *Developing the Leader Within You*, p. 125).

Jesus

God now turns to Plan A, Part 2, which is initiated by Christ during His earthly ministry. Jesus beautifully glorified God and made Him known by living His love. He said plainly,

> I have glorified thee on the earth, I have finished the work which thou gavest me to do. . . . I have manifest thy name [God's love] unto the men which thou gavest me out of the world. . . . And I have declared unto them they name, and will declare it, that the love wherewith thou hast loved me may be in them, and I in them. (John 15:4, 6, 26)

Jesus was attempting to raise up a new church that would carry out the same basic plan mapped out for Old Testament Israel. Some particulars have changed because He is no longer dealing with a literal nation in a specific geographic location. The Levites are no longer the only priests. The temple is longer limited to a building in Jerusalem. Now all Christians are priests and living temples wherever they are. Jerusalem is found wherever two or three have gathered together. The underlying focus of making God known through a community of love remains.

New Testament Church

As Jesus began phase two, He once again passed by the elite and initially chose a team of twelve teachable misfits. I can almost hear the onlooking universe crying, "Oh no, not again! Why do you choose so many difficult cases? You tried that in the Old Testament, and it didn't pan out all that great." But the power would clearly be from God. So Christ found His disciples and began shaping the Christian church. Paul reveals heaven's purpose:

> Unto him be glory in the church by Christ Jesus throughout all ages, world without end. (Ephesians 3:21)

Ellen White also makes it clear that the glory of God, His love, is still central:

> The Saviour turned from them [Israel] to entrust to others the privileges they had abused and the work they had slighted. God's glory must be revealed. The disciples were called to do the work that the Jewish leaders had failed to do. (*Acts of the Apostles,* p. 16)

As positive as the development of the New Testament church was, at the turn of the first century there were still issues to be clarified and areas of the globe to be loved. During the Middle Ages the church drifted so far from God's plan that His vision was nearly extinguished. Slowly, here and there, parts of the vision were eventually recovered—Luther, Melanchthon, Wesley, and others found key pieces. Finally, in 1844, God once again called attention to His original vision without being laughed to scorn. He presented a series of insights that paved the way for His love to become the central focus once again. He raised up the Seventh-day Adventist Church as Plan A, Part 3.

Reflection

What do you think were the main reasons the New Testament church could not sustain its initial success and eventually slipped into spiritual darkness?

Seventh-day Adventist Church

When God decided to raise up the Seventh-day Adventist Church, the onlooking universe was again dismayed at His tactics. He passed over the prestigious universities and seminaries, the great corporations and think tanks. Instead, one of the foremost members of His new team was an unknown teenager in Portland, Maine, who barely had a fourth-grade education and was in extremely poor health. I can hear the angels ask, "Did God say Ellen? Ellen Harmon? Not again! Every time the same thing, the weakest of the weak."

Central to the truths that God has given our church are the three angels' messages. The first angel's message places the glory of God once again at the center:

> And I saw another angel fly in the midst of heaven, having the everlasting gospel to preach unto them that dwell on the earth, and to every nation, and kindred, and tongue, and people. Saying with a loud voice, "Fear [honor] God, and give glory to Him, for the hour of his judgement is come, and worship Him that made heaven, and earth, and the sea, and the fountains of water. (Revelation 14:6-7)

The first angel's message focuses on God Himself in four ways:

1. The "gospel" is the good news about God.
2. Honor Him.
3. Give glory to Him.
4. Worship Him.

The paramount emphasis is once again on revealing the Godhead. Our church has been given the same fundamental charter that God gave ancient Israel, adapted to the times in which we live: To build a community of believers that draws others like a magnet to the extraordinary God revealed by their love.

> That which God purposed to do for the world through Israel, the chosen nation, He will finally accomplish through His church on earth today. (*Prophets and Kings,* p. 713, 714)

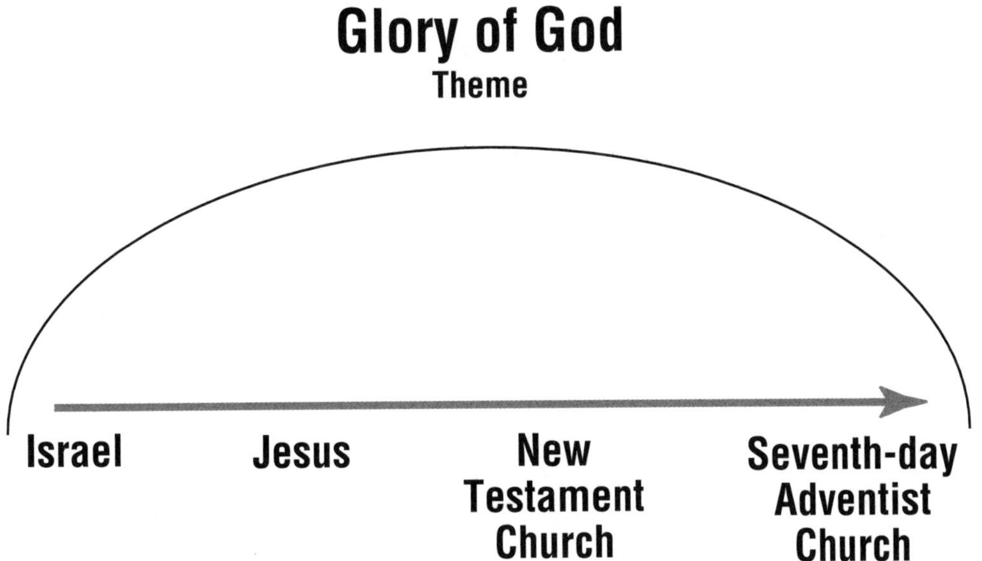

Unfortunately, we often fail to see how the first angel's message ties so beautifully into God's overall vision for His modern church.

> From the beginning it has been God's plan that through his church shall be reflected to the world His fulness and His sufficiency. The members of the church . . . are to show forth His glory. The church is the repository of the riches of the grace of Christ; and through the church will eventually be made manifest, even to "the principalities and powers in heavenly places," the final and full display of the love of God. (*Acts of the Apostles,* p. 9)

Ellen White clearly states what the primary burden of our message needs to be:

> It is the darkness of misapprehension of God that is enshrouding the world. Men are losing their knowledge of his character. At this time a message from God is to be proclaimed, a message illuminating in its influence and saving in its power. His character is to made known. Into the darkness of the world is to be shed the light of His glory, the light of His goodness, mercy, and truth. The last rays of merciful light, the last message of mercy to be given to the world, is a revelation of his character of love. (*Christ's Object Lessons,* p. 415, 416)

We might summarize the three angels' messages this way:

- First angel's message: Who God is.
- Second and third angels' messages (Babylon and the beast): Who God is not.
- Essentially, the overall messages are God and Not God.

Suppose we let gold represent the first angel's message and a Brillo scouring pad represent the second and third. I try to explain to you that gold is great and very valuable. However, I also tell you that there is counterfeit gold out there that people will try to foist on you. The counterfeits are the Brillo pads. Both pieces of information are important, but if I want you to take the gold, which message would I focus on the most, the gold or the Brillo pads? No contest. The gold, of course. My fear is that we can easily become people of the Brillo pad. We can become known more for our advanced "beastology" than for our obsession with the love of God.

Reflection

Why do you think it sometimes seems easier to dwell on end-time events more than the love of God?

There are many parallels between the way God worked with ancient Israel and how He works with the Adventist Church today. He has once again provided His people with incredible insights into many areas of life—education, family, health, biblical truth—to help hurting people find unparalleled wholeness. Once again, He is trying to create a new community through which people can become acquainted with His love. As God envisioned for Old Testament Israel, strangers should be breaking down Adventist church doors to discover our secret to successful living. Rick Warren writes,

> Quality produces quantity. A church full of genuinely changed people attracts others. If you study healthy churches you'll discover that when God finds a church that is doing a quality job of winning, nurturing, equipping, and sending out believers, He sends that church plenty of raw material. On the other hand, why would God send a lot of prospects to a church that doesn't know what to do with them? (*The Purpose-Driven Church,* Rick Warren, p. 51)

The Scriptures look forward to a time when God's love will truly receive top billing within Adventism and pour forth to a sin-sick world. "And after these things I saw another angel come down from heaven, having great power; and the earth was lightened with his glory" (Revelation 18:1). Our love should overflow and permeate every nook and cranny of society. As God planned for Israel, we should be the most well-known, most innovative, kindest church on the face of the earth.

God's amazing love is like a magnificent diamond with billions of facets. No one of us alone can fully reveal such infinite beauty. He does not expect us each to be little Christs. That is impossible since Jesus is infinite. But as each of us allows the Spirit of God to shine through our tiny facet of the diamond, the church can collectively reveal many aspects of that glory. Likewise, my left ear or right toe can't reflect all that I am (I hope!). It is similar to the pictures that are created when thousands of people in a stadium are given different cards to hold up at the same time. No one card is complete without the others.

God's portrait is terribly distorted through "rugged individualism." The kind of wholeness that reflects the Trinity best can only be provided by an accepting, nurturing community of love. And right here God's vision comes to a screeching halt because many of us have never learned how to be "church" in the biblical sense. We are taught much about how to be successful individual Christians. But seldom are we taught how to be Christians together.

Reflection

With regard to God's purpose for His church, which of Israel's missteps could local Adventist churches be repeating today?

So what has happened to God's vision for Adventism? Are we getting the big picture? One way to check on that is to ask what your church board and leaders talk about most often during meetings. Is most of their time taken up with whether or not to buy a new lawn mower, or are they wrestling with the truly big issues of how to be "church"? Are they mostly caught up with budget deficits, or are they studying how to fulfill God's vision? What story does the agenda tell?

Shortly after arriving at his new district, the pastor met with local church leaders to plan the future. "You folks have been members at this church for many years and know the needs best," the pastor began. "As you think about the big issues that confront us, as you think about God's plan for your church in this community, what do you feel we need to focus on most in the coming year? What are your top priorities?" One of the local elders shot up his hand. "Yes, Joe, what is at the top of your list?" the pastor asked. Joe leaned forward and shared earnestly, "Pastor, I feel there are far too many people in this church who drink coffee."

Drink coffee? Do I think it is a good idea to drink caffeine? No. But what a tragedy that this elder thought coffee was the biggest need he could envision. No doubt he had a severe case of tunnel vision, but I cannot totally write him off as an aberration. An Adventist friend and I were discussing how to witness to our community. He commented, "Well, my neighbors know what I stand for. They know I don't eat pork or work on Saturday." Are these important? Of course. The scary part was that my friend seemed satisfied that he had communicated the big picture, what he "stood for." Some of us have this dreadful habit of talking about individual trees as if they were the whole forest. Adventism should stand for something huge, exciting, positive. We should stand for knowing and revealing God.

Reflection

How often do your members and leaders talk about God's big vision for church? How can that theme receive greater emphasis?

We can certainly be thankful for all the good God has done through the Adventist church. Thousands of lives have been changed, including mine. The fact still remains, however, that God calls us Laodicea. That means that the church life we now see is not the church life that's going to be. Our doctrines are secure. But we will have to greatly lift our vision. We will have to take the principles discussed in the these lessons very seriously. What we often settle for is so little compared to God's vision for us.

Parable of the Shopping Spree

Imagine that a huge supermarket chooses your name out of the phone book to receive a free two-hour shopping spree The market sells a huge variety of fruits, vegetables, bakery goods, canned items, and packaged foods. You live in an inner city ghetto where most children have to miss breakfast. Your own six-member family often goes to bed hungry. Oh, how much good you could do!

On the morning of your big shopping spree you are picked up and chauffeured to the market in style. TV cameras are there ahead of you. A crowd has gathered. The store manager greets you warmly, reviews the rules, and shows you where to begin. You may keep as much food as you can get out the front door in two hours.

You get down in a runner's stance and test your sneakers for traction. The magic moment arrives, and off you go. The first thing you do is head straight to the familiar canned goods section. You grab a can of garden vegetable soup off the shelf, look at it with a satisfied smile, and race out the front door. You hold the can over your head in triumph and declare, "I'm all done!" You hug the stunned manager, wave to the crowd, and climb back into the store limousine for the journey home.

Is there anything wrong with a can of soup? No. But one measly can of soup is a tragic result when compared to what was available and to the huge needs back in the ghetto. Just imagine what could have been. God Himself has been thinking about what His church could have been for close to six thousand years. He has so much that He longs to share.

> It was my fifth year of pastoring. My two churches were doing reasonably well, and most people considered my ministry successful. For the first time I began seriously reading about God's vision for church and could occasionally hear a still, small voice calling me to a closer relationship with my church members and friends. Being a "rugged Yankee individualist," however, I secretly feared getting too close to people. Dependence on others was weakness. I hid behind a comfortable set of masks and defenses. I didn't consider myself a phony; I was just prudently self-protective. The voice got ignored.
>
> The Lord turned up the volume at that summer's camp meeting. When I ducked into a tent to escape the grueling sun during camp pitch, I found two other pastor friends. We shared ministerial woes, cataloging the ways our churches lacked Christlike love. Then the bombshell. One pastor said, "I've been convicted lately that I don't have that kind of love myself. How can we as pastors lead our people into something we haven't even experienced among ourselves?" Ouch. He had heard the same voice. A kindred spirit. Several days later eight pastors, including reluctant me, agreed to meet together once a week for twelve weeks with one item on the agenda—to learn how to love each other. One pastor we invited refused because he didn't see how it could help him get more baptisms.
>
> The next few weeks were a turning point in my life. They were uneasy at times but deeply rewarding. At the first pastoral group meeting we lifted our heads out of our foxholes slightly and surveyed the territory. During the second session everyone politely talked about the weather and the need for a raise (that generated a lot of discussion!). In the third session someone dared mention their loneliness and discouragement. It was acknowledged but largely ignored. "Holy men shouldn't talk about stuff like that," I thought on the way home. "Why doesn't he pray about it?" At the next meeting another pastor shared how he was still hurting from a nasty phone call from his head elder. Every pastor immediately reached for his Bible and we showered him with texts. Somehow he looked less than helped.
>
> It wasn't until later meetings that we were eventually able to let down our defenses, let go of our unholy jealousies, and begin to trust. I learned to say "I love you" in the group, without looking down. I learned I could be accepted just as I am. No one dug up dark, personal secrets. No one was interrogated. But we finally caught a glimpse of what the Bible really means by the word "church." We caught a new glimpse of God and the power of love. I had preached on these topics for years. I knew about them in my head. But now I knew about them in my heart.

Imagine the lives that God could touch if such blessings were duplicated throughout His church. Imagine what God could do if our church rediscovered its destiny. In Ephesians 2:21, the Apostle Paul tells us that God is trying to help His church become a "naos." Naos was the name for the Jewish temple, including the Most Holy Place. There God's glory and presence could be seen. Paul is telling us that church can be a place where people see the presence of God today. When non-Adventists experience the extraordinary love, acceptance, unity, fellowship, and kindness that flows from the membership, they will say, "God must be very much like you!"

We experience the life of God's new community in two's or three's, in small groups, and when we gather together Sabbath morning. Building such a community of faith will not produce a club of holy hermits. Instead, it will give enormous credibility to our words. It will also provide the vital healing environment from which believers can make a loving difference in their world. It is spiritual insecurity and preoccupation with externals that breeds saintly cliques. People who are secure in Christ are the only ones with enough love in their own cups to let it spill over to those around them.

Review Questions

1. "One of the things that fills my love cup the most is. . . ." (finish the sentence)

2. "The most meaningful way this group has helped me personally is. . . ." (finish the sentence)

3. During these Bible study lessons, what are the most significant ways your mental pictures of God and the church have changed?

4. What part of God's vision for the Seventh-day Adventist church excites you the most?

Love in Action

My Choice:

Pray specifically this week that God will send at least one person to you who very much needs a listening ear. Keep your radar up!

Your Choice:

Learning to be a Group: The best way to get others excited about small groups is through your own personal testimony.

Love in Action Feedback: What hurting person were you able to carefully listen to this week?

Ice Breaker: As you look back over the past 16 weeks, what has been the most memorable moment or experience in this group for you?

The Value of Vision

Last week I tried to buy concert tickets at the last minute to hear Beethoven's stirring Ninth Symphony. Unfortunately, they were all sold out. The day of the concert I alternated between mild regret and a good old-fashioned melancholy funk. Then, about 3:00 p.m., a friend called out of the blue and asked if my wife and I would like two free tickets to that very same concert. His wife had taken ill at the last minute and couldn't make it. Nothing serious, just a touch of the flu. I expressed sympathy, then shared the exciting news with my classical-music-relishing better half. The tickets were fourth row, main floor. I could see the beads of sweat on the conductor's brow. As the orchestra, the one-hundred-voice choir, and the four vocal soloists blended magnificently to create waves of great music, my mind couldn't help but think once again about God's spiritual orchestra, the church. Tears nearly welled up in my eyes as I pictured what the church could become if we only understood God's dream and committed to pursuing it together. That vision is never far from my thoughts. Have you ever glanced at the sun, turned away, and seen sunspots everywhere? That is what has happened to me since staring carefully at God's plan.

Has that vision gripped your own heart? Has it ever kept you awake at night trying to think God's thoughts after Him? Our churches are supposed to be vibrant centers of love that make a dramatic, positive impact on their communities. Seventh-day Adventism is supposed to be a household word throughout the world, known for our ability to transform lives and nurture hurting people to wholeness and maturity in Christ. Thank God for what we do have as a denomination, but heaven is trying desperately to lift our vision and open our eyes to thrilling new possibilities. Unless a local church is gripped by God's vision, there is not much point in tinkering around the edges. Understanding and committing to that vision are at the core of lasting renewal. A church's highest priority should be discovering how God wants them to live out His dream in their community.

The Scriptures tell us, "Where there is no vision the people perish" (Proverbs 29:18). In the absence of a clear, captivating vision, the local church usually develops negative traits.

- Morale suffers,
- tradition dominates,
- infighting nibbles away at unity,
- a fortress mentality evolves,
- members are largely spectators,
- people major in minors,

- busyness replaces a real sense of ministry.

Lynn Anderson describes what happens when people lose their vision:

> A group of pilgrims landed on the shores of America about 370 years ago. With great vision and courage they had come to settle in the new land. In the first year, they established a town. In the second, they elected a town council. In the third, the government proposed building a road five miles westward into the wilderness. But in the fourth year, the people tried to impeach the town council because the people thought such a road into the forest was a waste of public funds. Somehow these forward-looking people had lost their vision. Once able to see across oceans, they now could not look five miles into the wilderness. (*Developing The Leader Within You,* John Maxwell, p. 136)

An old Chinese proverb says, "Unless you change direction, you are likely to arrive at where you are headed" (*Visionary Leadership*, Burt Nanus, p. 3).

Too many churches are like this family:

> One day father gathers the family around him in the living room and declares, "Hey, I figured out what we can do for summer vacation. Let's go for a nice, long three-week drive!" The family doesn't seem particularly excited. The disappointment on Dad's face is obvious as his wife, Donna, and their three kids respond, "Do we have to? Can't we just sit around and watch TV? Can't we just take it easy?" But Dad insists. They should all go for a long drive.
>
> The next day, while the family watches, Dad packs the food, sleeping bags, tent, lantern, clothes and, most importantly, the map. On the day of departure, Dad forces everyone out of bed, badgers them to get dressed, and heaps on the guilt in order to get them into the car. "Now, this will be a great vacation. I just know it," Dad intones. "So, where shall we go?" he continues. "Hey, Donna, look at this neat road right here on the map. Let's follow that for a while." So the car speeds west on route 28 for about five hours through increasingly unfamiliar scenery. After a lunch break, Dad drags everyone back inside the cramped auto. "Hey, kids, look at this pretty red road on the map," he offers. "Let's take that one." Another five grueling hours.
>
> For the next three weeks Dad zigs and zags from one colorful road to the next, depending on what looks interesting to him at the time. "Here's a highway on the map that has an unusual squiggle," he says, "and look how this one is shaped like a fish hook. Let's try it." Sometimes Dad goes back and forth over a road he especially likes several times. Up and down hills, through countless, boring little towns and zillions of traffic lights, pulling up at dozens of toll booths, gas stations, and rest areas, stopping over and over for directions. Three weeks later, when they finally pull into the driveway back home, Dad has racked up an amazing 10,000 miles and expended every ounce of energy cajoling, urging, prodding, and soothing disgruntled family members. The kids have either fought or been rowdy almost all the way. No one looks forward to next year.

How different that vacation could have been if they shared a captivating vision about some exciting destination. Imagine a new scene with a different family.

> This father gathers the family around, and they all decide, "Let's spend our vacation going to the Grand Canyon. When we get there we can ride the mules down to the bottom of the canyon and explore!" Though the finances will be tight and the old car will groan all the way, what an adventure it will be. How much prodding and urging do you think will be necessary this time?

Although both families put on many miles, there is a huge difference between "going for a drive" and "visiting the Grand Canyon." Churches too often find themselves zigging and zagging from one interesting program and activity to the next with no sense of purpose. What a difference a captivating vision can make!

"There is no more powerful engine driving an organization toward excellence and long-range success than an attractive, worthwhile, and achievable vision of the future, widely shared" (*Visionary Leadership*, Burt Nanus, p. 186). In the presence of such a vision the church can thrive. Vision is a powerful force for good.

Remember when the recent changes came to the Soviet Union? Remember Boris Yeltsin standing on a tank addressing thousands, saying, "We will never go back, never!" The Russian people had tasted what we in America wake up to every day—democracy. Several years from now some university professor will ask her students to pick out the dates in the past 500 years that have affected world history the most. One of those dates would have to be 1991, when the shackles of communism were lifted from the lives of millions. And how was this accomplished? For the people of Russia, it all started with a dream.

The following graphic depicts the value of vision. Study it carefully with the explanation that follows.

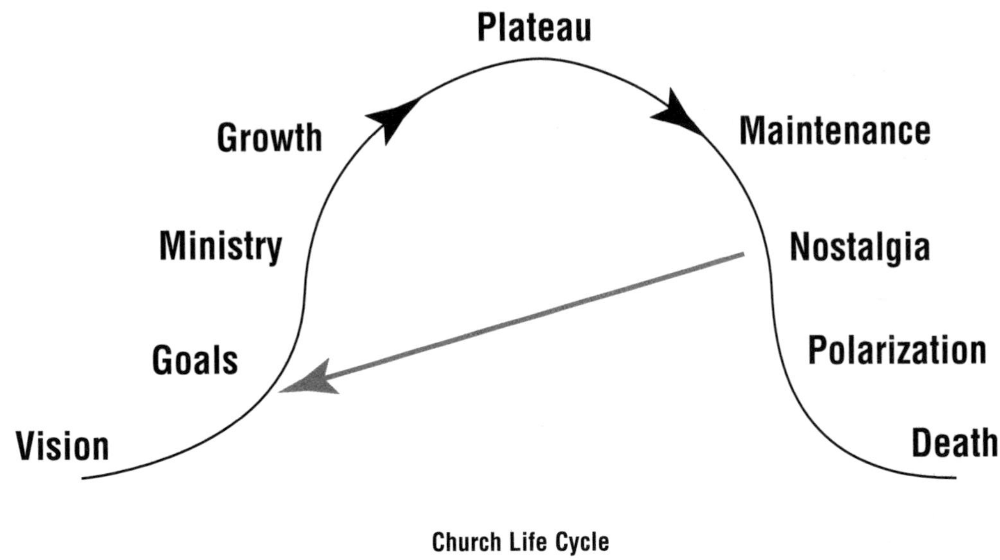

Church Life Cycle

(Modified from *Reviving the Plateaued Church*, R. D. Baker, Truman Brown, Jr., Robert Dale, p. 6)

Local congregations usually begin with a small group of people who have a **vision** for starting a church in their area. They set **goals**, organize for **ministry**, and **growth** results. Perhaps, after several years, the church unfortunately **plateaus** and may settle into a **maintenance** mode. Not too awful, but not too exciting either. They begin sliding down the slippery slope. There may be no decline in numbers, but spiritually things are slowly rotting from within. Next, **nostalgia** sets in and the members begin to recount the "good old days." "Remember when we used to get big crowds for Ingathering?" "Remember when the youth used to turn out in droves for Friday night MV?" The members may then become **polarized** by forming little cliques. The church is like spiritual swiss cheese, full of holes. The building is still standing. The people still come every week. They still hold VBS and cooking schools, but the vitality has drained away. Church is predictable. They are nearing spiritual **death**.

The problem is usually that the old vision has faded and lost its power. The wrong approach is to try and climb back up the slippery slope. The answer is to go back to **vision** and discover God's dream for your church once again. It is the role of local leadership to be "custodians of the vision," to make sure it is understood, relevant, and consistent with the principles and priorities in these lessons. Effective leaders shape methods to fit God's purposes. A captivating vision should be the North Star by which a congregation charts its course. Such a vision can keep churches from plateauing and provide the impetus for continued health and growth.

Reflection

Where do you think your own local church is now on the Church Life Cycle chart? Why do you feel that way?

All the great events in Scripture began with someone or some group of people in whom God implanted a dream. Nehemiah is typical of many Bible visionaries. He stepped forward at a critical time in the life of Israel. The Jewish people had been dragged into Babylonian captivity in 587 B.C. They were humiliated and disgraced by their enemies. The future looked hopeless. Amidst such difficulty, Nehemiah chose to believe the apparently impossible dream that Jerusalem could be restored. Besides this spiritual giant, there are many other men and women of large vision and commitment, such as Joseph, David, Daniel, Mary, Peter, Paul, and John.

But the greatest visionary of all is Christ. When He gives the disciples their marching orders in Acts 1:8, I can imagine them listening intently as He says, "You will receive power when the Holy Spirit comes to you." The disciples are interested. Jesus continues, "And you will be my witnesses in Jerusalem, and in all Judea." So far, so good. They can do that. Then the vision gets bigger when Jesus adds, "and Samaria." They are supposed to minister to their enemies? The vision is growing significantly. Then Jesus pulls back the curtain on the full dimensions of His dramatic plan: "You will bring my love to the very ends of the earth!" What a dream for this little band of eleven to contemplate. What a captivating vision for this motley group that has never traveled more than a hundred miles from home. "To the ends of the earth!" No one has ever out-dreamed God.

Ellen White urged believers, "Bring your minds up to the greatness of the work. Your narrow plans, your limited ideas, are not to come into your methods of working" (*Evangelism*, p. 553).

A clear vision can become the basis for ongoing feedback and accountability. Rick Warren writes, "How does a church evaluate itself? Not by comparing itself to other churches, but by asking, 'Are we doing what God intends for us to do?' and 'How well are we doing it?' According to Peter Drucker, the two most critical questions for evaluating your church are: "'What is our business?' and 'How's business?'" (*The Purpose-Driven Church*, Rick Warren, p. 93).

> How important is it to know what business you are in? The United States railroads are a historic example. How different the world would be if the railroads had understood the business they were in. Unfortunately, most of the U.S. railroad companies thought they were in the "railroad business." That was fine as long as there were no highways, automobiles, or airplanes. It was a great business to be in as long as the West was expanding and the best way to travel was by rail.
>
> But today many of the U.S. railroads are almost out of business or highly subsidized. The reason? They failed to see their real business. The railroad companies were not in the railroad business. They were in the transportation business. Failure to realize this led to the demise of much of the railroad system in the United States.
>
> Travel in the United States today would be quite different had the railroads defined their business as transportation. If they had, there would no doubt be transportation centers—large hubs of interconnected systems—in the United States today. Our whole world of travel would be different. (*Moving The Church Into Action,* Kent Hunter, p. 53-54)

Many churches think they are in the "evangelistic meeting" and "cooking school" business. They think they are in the "Sabbath school" or the "worship service" business. That is not really true. That is like saying we are in the railroad business. Fundamentally, at its core, the church is in the "people business." We are in the business of building people to the glory of God and loving them to Christian maturity, as we studied in the previous lesson. As Rick Warren has observed, "Instead of trying to grow a church with programs, focus on growing people with a process" (*The Purpose-Driven Church*, p. 108). Church is supposed to be a "people garden."

> Imagine a tribe of people who have never heard about airplanes. Somehow they stumble across a gleaming, intact 737 cargo aircraft that was downed in bad weather without anyone noticing. The pilots have headed north on foot for help. The tribal leaders spend days trying to figure out what all the dials and gadgets in the cockpit are for. Soon they accidentally start the twin jet engines, then scramble outside in terror at the horrific noise. After regaining their courage, they return and shut the engines down. Through experimentation, these clever people learn to steer the plane up and down the local roads with the engines revved and blaring. They find extra fuel on board and turn the aircraft into a kind of Greyhound bus for the townspeople, making several runs each week along the dirt streets. They even make a schedule, with pre-arranged stops at the mango grove, the beach, the water hole, and center of town. The plane is useful, but far from fulfilling the purpose for which it was designed. You see, what we expect is often what we get. The mental model or picture we have in our heads of why something was made determines how it is used.
>
> The same can be true of church. Many congregations have unwittingly turned their local church into a bus, when they should be climbing to 30,000 feet. The members are relatively content because that is all they know. They try to find ways to make the bus run faster and get more miles per gallon. They offer community programs to get more people to ride the bus. But they never imagine that their mental concept of what church is supposed to be may need a fundamental overhaul. They don't know that church life is limited by their distorted vision of why church was created in the first place.

The following graphic depicts two very different perspectives on the purpose of church—the Information Model and the Glory Of God Model. In a sense, they are the bus and the airplane. Which model your congregation adopts will probably be the most important choice they will ever make; all the rest is commentary. The model they choose will largely determine how they "do church." Most churches make their choice more by default than by a deliberate process. The effects of that choice are just as pervasive nonetheless.

Certain fruit, or logical consequences, develop from the two root orientations. These are listed in sequence on each side from the bottom up. The consequences develop one after the other in a cause/effect fashion. As you move up the two lists, notice that each item is listed across from its contrasting pair. It will take a little extra effort to study the two models, but the issues are too important to miss. Please look over the graphic, then refer back to it as you read the explanation that follows.

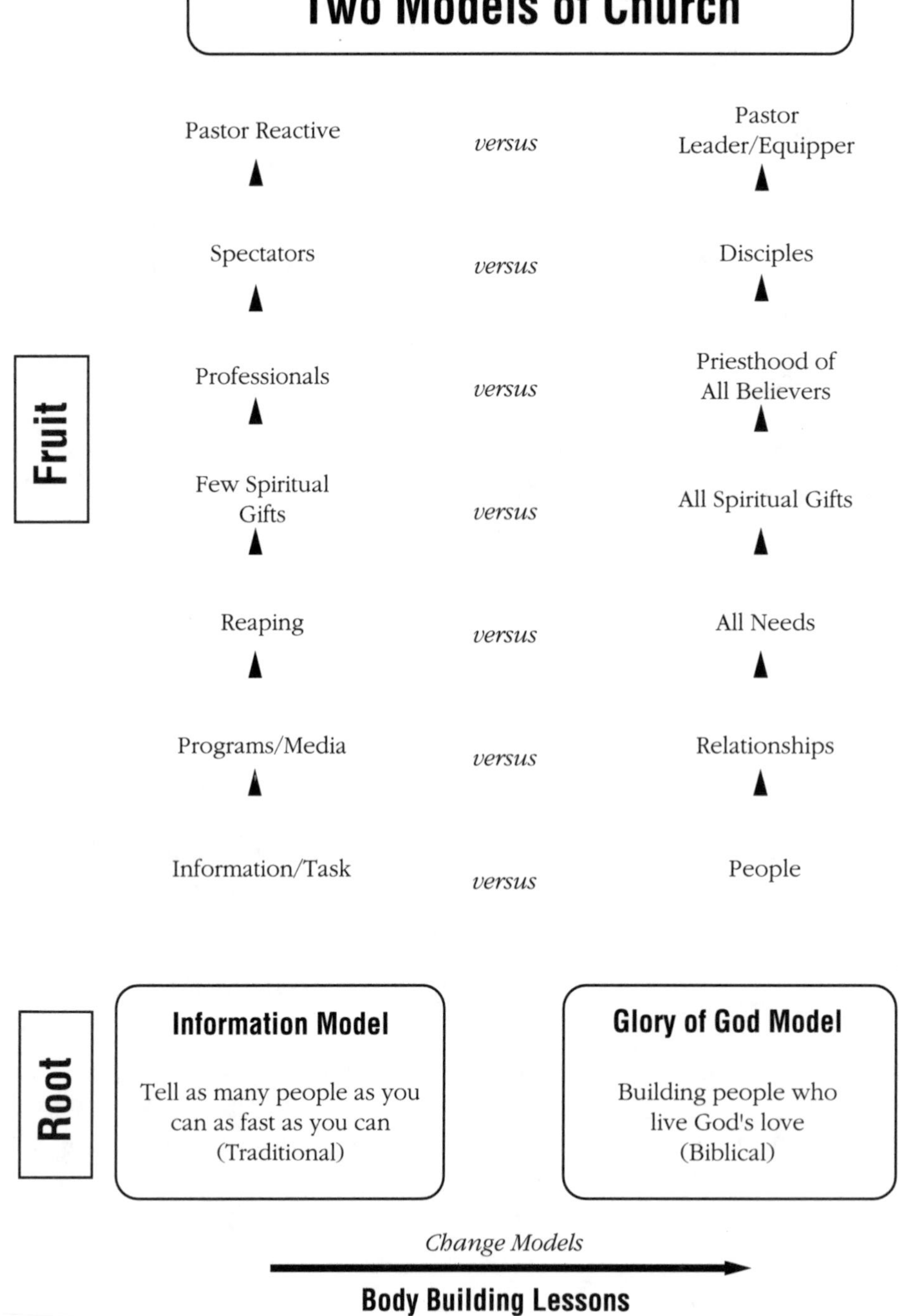

The Information Model (refer to "Two Models" chart above)

On the left is the Information Model of church. It puts primary emphasis on **spreading correct biblical information** to as many people as we can, as fast as we can. This church sees its main purpose as preaching and teaching the Gospel, the three angels' messages, and other truths. Out of that perspective there emerges the following list of priorities and consequences, the fruit:

- Information/Task—Information sharing becomes the primary goal. We may not describe such an emphasis in this way, but our actions indicate our priorities.
- Programs/Media—It is logical, then, to depend more and more on methods that will get the information out the fastest, such as mass media and programs.
- Reaping—Getting people to say yes to the information and accept it becomes our major focus, so reaping or getting decisions is paramount.
- Few spiritual gifts—The heavy emphasis on information sharing and reaping leaves many people with planting, sowing, and nurturing gifts out in the cold, feeling like they don't fit in or are not valued.
- Professionals—We increasingly depend on the religious professionals (pastors, evangelists, etc) who can explain the information best.
- Spectators—The members then develop a spectator mentality because they do not see themselves as vital to success.
- Pastor Reactive—Because the many gifts of the Spirit are not activated, the ministry load falls squarely on the pastor's shoulders. He adopts a reactive mode, like a plumber who spends all day fixing leaks.

All of these consequences flow logically and tragically from the underlying paradigm of the Information Model of church. Information (biblical truth) is of course vital, but it is a means to an end, not an end in itself. This model is not "wrong." It is simply far too narrow, and such an imbalance can have a very negative affect on church life. God has a much larger vision in mind.

The Glory Of God Model

The Glory of God Model emphasizes building people to the glory of God; that is, people who the Spirit enables to love. It is about biblical disciple making. It includes biblical information and truth to be sure, but so much more. The positive consequences and priorities that flow out of this very different model include these:

- People—Building people becomes the key to being church. The emphasis is not only on what we know but, more importantly, on who we are. It is broad, holistic, and balanced.
- Relationships—The ultimate focus is squarely on relationships, within the church and without.
- All needs—We are now interested in meeting whatever needs people may have in order to help them become whole.
- All spiritual gifts—In order to meet the great variety of people needs we must activate all the gifts of the Spirit.
- Priesthood of all believers—Activating all the gifts means that we must take seriously the vital biblical teaching of priesthood of all believers.
- Disciples—Because of the emphasis on holism and everyone being a priest, our goal becomes not just baptisms but producing mature disciples for Christ.
- Pastor Leader/Equipper—Now that the gifts and ministries of the laity are activated, the pastor can become the specialist God designed as leader/equipper.

It is the Glory of God Model that captures the biblical vision best. Notice that it is rather useless to try to change one of the fruit from the left side of the "Two Models" chart to the right side without first changing the fundamental that is in people's heads. For instance, at one point in my pastoral ministry I tried to take a shortcut by going directly across from "few spiritual gifts" to "all spiritual gifts." I saw that not many of my members were utilizing their gifts. So I launched into spiritual gift seminars and tried to place them in ministry. Things improved for a while, but eventually drifted back, like a rubber band that has been stretched out and then released. What went wrong? I had changed the method without first changing their fundamental vision of what church was all about. I tacked on new fruit without changing the root.

Unless we alter people's underlying values and philosophy, change will not make much sense and will be seen as either a threat or just one more transient program. These lessons and small-group experience are specifically designed to help people shift the roots of their thinking from the Information Model to the more complete Glory of God Model. Studying and understanding the "Two Models" chart can give you a very important orientation toward the new vision that God seeks to instill.

> Suppose we compare these two church models to a trip to Florida or California. Journeying to Florida will represent the Information Model and traveling to California will represent the Glory of God Model. If we are starting out from Boston, Massachusetts, we have to make a fundamental decision before beginning: are we going to head south or west? That is the critical choice. I could be making great time motoring along a highway, but what real difference does that make if I should be headed in an entirely different direction? Activity alone is not an accurate measure of success. Suppose a committee is formed that works very hard figuring out how to save money on motels and restaurants all down the East Coast. What good will all that labor do if I should be headed to California? Has your church ever intentionally decided which way it is headed? Are all your church's activities contributing to getting you there?

Reflection

> In general, which of the two models of church (Information or Glory of God) has your congregation adopted? Where are you at currently in your own thinking? How has people's root understanding of church affected church life locally?

Over the past several weeks you have spent time with fellow Adventists discovering various aspects of God's vision for His people. At this point, group members often want to know what to do from here. The first and best place to begin is with yourself. I used to say, "Why doesn't somebody do something?" and then I realized that I *am* somebody. It is easy to think that things would be better if others would only change. I have found the most effective strategy is to ask myself, "What can I do? What little things can I begin doing or saying that will make a difference?" Here are some possibilities:

1. You can personalize the principles and vision your group has uncovered by developing your own Personal Mission Statement. Such a statement captures on paper how you want to make a difference and how you want to incorporate the insights from these lessons into your everyday life. In his best-selling book, *The Seven Habits of Highly Effective People*, Stephen Covey talks about how to create your own Personal Mission Statement:

> In your mind's eye, see yourself going to the funeral of a loved one. Picture yourself driving to the funeral parlor or chapel, parking the car, and getting out. As you walk inside the building, you notice the flowers, the soft organ music. You see the faces of friends and family you pass along the way. You feel the shared sorrow of losing, the joy of having known, that radiates from the hearts of the people there.
>
> As you walk down to the front of the room and look inside the casket, you suddenly come face to face with yourself. This is your funeral, three years from today.
>
> As you take a seat and wait for the services to begin, you look at the program in your hand. There are to be four speakers. The first is from your family, immediate and also extended. The second speaker is one of your friends, someone who can give a sense of what you were as a person. The third speaker is from your work or profession. And the fourth is from your church.

Now think deeply. What would you like each of these speakers to say about you and your life? What difference would you like to have made in their lives? (*The Seven Habits of Highly Effective People,* Stephen Covey, Jr., p. 96-97)

These four aspects of your life, along with any others you may wish to include, form the framework for your Personal Mission Statement. After identifying all the major life roles you want to target, list two or three results, or goals, that are important to you in each area. My own list of life roles includes Christian, husband, father, son, church member, employee, friend. My Personal Mission Statement begins with the following two roles and goals, which I review regularly:

Husband:

- To let my wife know how important she is to me by expressing affection and having regular dates together.
- To listen carefully to her needs.
- To encourage and support her own personal development.

Father:

- To pay more attention to modeling values than talking about them.
- To laugh often together.
- To take more time to talk as friends.

2. You can become a missionary to your own church. Model the caring and kindness that come from knowing you are loved. Share some of what you have learned in these lessons with another person. Pray that God will lead you to people who are open to understanding His vision.

3. Invite someone to a small group that studies these truths and principles. Offer to go with them if necessary. Stay connected with those who long to make God's vision a reality by getting together periodically.

4. Look for some area of church life, big or small, where you can use your spiritual gifts and talents to help implement some aspect of God's vision. It is better to light a candle than to curse the darkness.

John Richardson once said,

When it comes to the future, there are three kinds of people:

those who let it happen,

those who make it happen,

and those who wonder what happened.

Hopefully you will be among the group that is determined, by God's grace, to make it happen.

Ah, great it is to believe the dream,
As we stand in youth by the starry stream.
But a greater thing is to live life through,
And say at the end, the dream came true.

(*Developing The Leader Within You*, John Maxwell, p. 140)

Review Questions

1. For this week's group meeting, begin working on your Personal Mission Statement. Choose at least one role and two or three related goals. Share them with the group.

2. Look over the following list of "vision killers" and discuss which ones you think may arise in your church and how you might deal with them.
   - Tradition
   - Fear
   - Complacency
   - Criticism
   - Short-term thinking

3. What needs to be done in your church to get started on the process of implementing the principles you learned in this group? How can you "get going"?

Notes

Notes

Notes

Notes